DAVID WILLIAMSON was ...
brought up in Bairnsdale, no...
graduate in Mechanical Engi...
sity and was a lecturer in therm...
ogy at Swinburn Institute of Technology until ...
full-length play, *The Coming of Stork,* had its premiere at the
La Mama Theatre, Carlton, in 1970 and later became the
film *Stork*, directed by Tim Burstall.

But it was his next two plays which together established
him as Australia's most sought-after dramatic writer. *The
Removalists* and *Don's Party,* both written in 1971, were quickly
taken up and performed around Australia, then in London
and later made into films with screenplays by the author. *The
Removalists* won the British George Devine Award in 1971 for
the Nimrod Street production in Sydney; and in 1972 the Australian Writers Guild Awgie Awards for the best stage play
and the best script in any medium. In 1973 David Williamson was nominated the most promising playwright by the London *Evening Standard* following the British production of *The
Removalists.*

The next play was *Jugglers Three* (1972) commissioned by
the Melbourne Theatre Company; followed by *What If You
Died Tomorrow* (1973) for the Old Tote Theatre Company;
The Department (1975) and *A Handful of Friends* (1976) for the
South Australian Theatre Company. *The Club* (1977) broke
all previous box office records and in 1978 had seasons at the
Kennedy Centre, Washington, on Broadway and in Berlin.
In 1980 the Nimrod Theatre production went to London. The
film, directed by Bruce Beresford, was released in 1980. *Travel-
ling North* was performed round Australia in 1979 and in London in 1980 and the film version will be released in 1987. It
was followed by *Celluloid Heroes* (1980), *The Perfectionist* (1982),
Sons of Cain (1985) and *Emerald City* (1987). Production of the
film version of *Emerald City* will also commence during 1987.

David Williamson has won the Australian Film Institute
film script award for *Petersen* (1974), *Don's Party* (1976) and
Gallipoli (1981). Recent scripts include *Phar Lap,* the TV mini-
series *The Last Bastion* and the telemovie *The Perfectionist.* He
lives in Sydney with his journalist wife Kristin and four
children.

By the same author

EMERALD CITY

David Williamson

CURRENCY PRESS • SYDNEY

CURRENCY PLAYS

General Editor: Katharine Brisbane

First published in 1987 by
Currency Press Pty Ltd.,
P.O. Box 452 Paddington, N.S.W. 2021,
Australia, in the Current Theatre Series.
This edition May, 1987.

National Library of Australia
Cataloguing-in-Publication data
Williamson, David
  Emerald City

  ISBN 0 86819 170 1

  I. Title.

A822'.3

Typeset by Love Computer Typesetting, Sydney
Printed by Southwood Press Pty Limited, Sydney, N.S.W.

Currency's creative writing program is assisted by the Literature Board of the Australia
Council, the Federal Government's arts funding and advisory body.

Introduction

Even for David Williamson *Emerald City* must have broken a record. Within four months of its premiere five separate productions had opened around Australia; and a return season in Sydney, followed by an interstate tour, was contracted.

After sixteen years, a new Williamson play is greeted by the theatre-going public with singular anticipation. He is still the most bankable name in the business; and the source of his popularity is his ability to combine an unwavering curiosity about the familiar with an undiminished facility to surprise. Audiences know they can rely upon a Williamson play to be entertaining, accessible, and appropriate to the mood of the moment.

And *Emerald City* did not disappoint them. It is one of his cleverest comedies — sharp-edged, satirical, and accusatory, it lays into the materialism of the eighties with a razor wit and a saving recognition that the author himself is first in the firing line.

Despite the unanimous box office verdict, the play has caused sharp divisions in its audiences. Such divisions have been a continuing response to Williamson's writing — intrinsic to his purpose in capturing a general concern within an immediate and personal one.

Emerald City, it would appear, is the confession of a successful script writer and his literary wife as they encounter the fleshpots of Sydney and compete for a harbour view. It extends to become a satirical portrait of a materialist, frivolous city in which the sensitive and talented find themselves lonely, unappreciated and finally seduced by the superficial attractions and ostentatious wealth. From another viewpoint *Emerald City* is an indictment — just as *The Department* was in 1975, just as *The Removalists* was back in 1971 and *Sons of Cain* last year — of gifted people who debase their talents, of class and corporate leaders who deny their moral responsibilities.

It is a theme which has haunted the contemporary Australian theatre — not only in Williamson's work but in Patrick White's *Big Toys;* and the plays of Louis Nowra and Stephen Sewell in particular.

It is the theme preached by the historian Manning Clark, of a country which has lost its faith — or rather has discarded the religious faith imposed by its former masters; but which lacks the moral resources to realise its own dilemma.

David Williamson's saving grace remains his capacity to be shocked. After fifteen years in the commercial world he still retains the innocent eye and the active conscience. Colin Rogers embodies the classic middle-class dilemma of the eighties, the decade of Mad Max, Les Patterson and Crocodile Dundee, when for the first time in our history our national character is in the mass market:

> 'The money men won't look at anything', says Kate 'that's not sex, sadism or sensation.' 'That's the *excuse* I use to justify what I'm doing', replies Colin, 'but honestly, isn't it just that? An excuse. A justification? Couldn't I fight harder?' (p. 53)

And then again:

> 'What do you have at the end of your life to show for your artistic success? An old age pension, a one bar radiator — if you can afford the fuel bills — and a few yellowing crits in a dusty scrapbook. It's too demeaning, Kate. It's too bloody demeaning! If I've got to choose between money and oblivion, I'll take the money!' (p. 56)

'Why are the pricks so greedy?' is the cry of Kevin, the crusading editor, fighting for the little people in Williamson's last play, *Sons of Cain.* Under the comedy *Emerald City* goes further. Under the jibes, the fun and the jokes about the television industry the author remains shocked and impotent, contemplating the fresh revelation that greed is not the prerogative of the politicians, the corporations or organised crime; its roots are the ingrained selfishness common to all of us.

Katharine Brisbane

Above: Mariette Rups-Donnelly as Kate and Robert van
Mackelenberg as Colin in the Hole in the Wall production.
Photo by Peter Flanagan   Below: Robyn Nevin as Kate
and John Bell as Colin in the Sydney Theatre Company
production. Photo by Branco Gaica

Above: Max Cullen as Mike and Dennis Grosvenor as Malcolm in the Sydney Theatre Company production. Photo by Branco Gaica. Below: Tina Williamson as Helen and Rod Langlands as Mike in the Hole in the Wall Theatre Company production, Perth. Photo by Peter Flanagan.

Robyn Nevin as Kate in the Sydney Theatre Company production.
Photo by Branco Gaica

Above: John Bell as Colin and Max Cullen as Mike in the Sydney Theatre Company production. Photo by Branco Gaica. Below: Rosemary Barr as Elaine in the Hole in the Wall production. Photo by Peter Flanagan

Emerald City was first performed by the Sydney Theatre Company at the Drama Theatre of the Sydney Opera House on 1 January 1987, with the following cast:

COLIN	John Bell
ELAINE	Ruth Cracknell
KATE	Robyn Nevin
MIKE	Max Cullen
HELEN	Andrea Moor
MALCOLM	Dennis Grosvenor

Directed by Richard Wherrett
Designed by Laurence Eastwood

CHARACTERS

COLIN, a scriptwriter, forty-ish
ELAINE, his agent, fifty
KATE, a publisher, Colin's wife, forty-ish
MIKE, an entrepreneur, forties
HELEN, a PR consultant, late twenties
MALCOLM, a merchant banker, forties

Ruth Cracknell as Elaine in the Sydney Theatre Company production. Photo by Branco Gaica.

ACT ONE

COLIN *stands by a window, gazing out. He is a handsome, engaging man in his late thirties whose natural disposition is warm and open, though when he feels uncertain or under attack, he's capable of an aloof, almost arrogant air and of sharp retaliation. He is watched by* ELAINE ROSS, *a shrewd capable woman in her fifties.*

COLIN: [*turning away from the window*] What other city in the world could offer a view like this?

ELAINE: Rio. But I'm prepared to believe it's the second most beautiful city in the world.

COLIN: I used to come here when I was a kid and go back with my head full of images of lushness. Green leaves spilling over sandstone walls, blue water lapping at the sides of ferries. Flame trees, Jacaranda, heavy rain, bright sun.

ELAINE: [*drily*] Yes, there's no lack of colour.

COLIN: Everything in Melbourne is flat, grey, parched and angular. And everything is controlled and *moderate*. It never rains in buckets like it does here in Sydney, it drizzles. The wind never gusts, it creeps along the streets like a wizened old mugger and slips a blade into your kidneys. Sydney has always felt like a city of sub-tropical abundance.

ELAINE: Abundance. [*Nodding*] Yes. There's abundance. Sometimes I'm not sure of what.

COLIN: There's a hint of decadence too, but to someone from the puritan south, even that's appealing.

ELAINE: I didn't drag you up here, then?

COLIN: No, I would've come years ago, but I couldn't persuade Kate. She's convinced Sydney is full of con men, crooks and hustlers.

ELAINE: She's right.

COLIN: Melbourne has its quota of shysters.

ELAINE: Sydney is different. Money *is* more important here.

COLIN: Why more so than Melbourne?

ELAINE: To edge yourself closer to a view. In Melbourne all views are equally depressing, so there's no point.

COLIN: [*laughing*] I'm not convinced.

ELAINE: It's true. No one in Sydney ever wastes time debating the meaning of life — it's getting yourself a water frontage. People devote a lifetime to the quest. You've come to a city that knows what it's about, so be warned. The only ethic is that there are no ethics, loyalties rearrange themselves daily, treachery is called acumen and honest men are called fools.

COLIN: I thought you liked the place?

ELAINE: I do. It's my city and I accept it for what it is. Just don't behave as if you're still in Melbourne, because if you do you'll get done like a dinner.

> [ELAINE *exits.* COLIN *moves thoughtfully to centre stage.* KATE *walks on. She's* COLIN*'s wife. An attractive, vivacious and intelligent woman in her thirties. Her frowning earnestness often makes her funny when she's not trying to be.*]

COLIN: This is an amazing city.

KATE: [*bluntly*] I hate it.

COLIN: [*suddenly angry*] Christ, Kate! If you're going to be this negative right from the start, let's just cancel everything and go back south.

KATE: We can't. You insulted everybody as soon as you knew we were going.

COLIN: It's a stunning city, Kate. You should see the view that Elaine's got.

KATE: To judge a city by the views it offers is the height of superficiality. This city is *dreadful*. The afternoon paper had three words on the cover: 'Eel Gets Chop', and no matter how much I juggle that around in my mind I can't find a meaning that justifies the whole front page of a newspaper.

COLIN: To judge a city by *one* afternoon newspaper is also the height of superficiality.

KATE: *All* the media here is devoted to trivia. The places to be seen dining in, the clothes to be seen wearing, the films to be seen seeing — it's all glitter and image and style. New York without the intellect.

COLIN: What's Melbourne? Perth without the sunshine?

KATE: People in Melbourne care about more than the image they project.

COLIN: They seem just as eager for money and fame as anyone is.

KATE: My friends don't care about money and fame. Terri works her guts out in the Western suburbs helping kids fight their way out of intellectual and physical poverty. Sonia tries to repair the psyches of wives whose husbands beat the Christ out of them, and Steve uses his legal skills to try and stop the powerless being ripped off by the powerful —

COLIN: [*interrupting*] Have you ever seen any of them laugh? Wait, I'm wrong. I have. When one of Sonia's battered wives sliced off her husband's member. She had quite a chuckle over that one. And she didn't want the wife to go to prison because it was only a 'one off' act.

KATE: They might have tunnel vision in some areas —

COLIN: [*interrupting*] Some areas? That lot are so paranoid they blame the C.I.A. if the weather turns cloudy!

KATE: At least they don't live their lives totally for themselves.

COLIN: You know what I couldn't stand about them? Their smug self-righteousness. They were all earning salaries five times the size of any of the poor bastards they were supposed to be helping.

KATE: All right. You didn't like them. I did.

COLIN: I have heard Terri laugh too, come to think of it. When I fractured my elbow tripping over that clump of wheezing fur she claims is a cat.

KATE: They used to laugh a lot. Just not when you were around.

COLIN: What's that meant to mean?

KATE: You picked a fight with them every time they opened their mouths.

COLIN: Can you blame me? They made it quite clear they despised the films I'd written.

KATE: Colin, you're paranoid.

COLIN: They despised them. My scripts were about the lives of middle-class trendies. The truth was *they* were the biggest middle-class trendies of the lot. Steve managed to hate my films without ever *seeing* one.

KATE: [*laughing*] Colin, you're totally paranoid.

COLIN: [*Agitated that she won't believe him, impassioned*] He told me with immense pride that he'd never seen an Australian film in his life, and that in the last ten years he'd never seen a film that didn't have subtitles. How trendy can you get? How many working-class Australians drink vintage wine every night of the week like that lot did? How many working-class Australians go to listen to Hungarian string quartets? How many working-class Australians find the neo-realist fabulism of the South American novel 'sadly passe'. Those friends of yours were right on the cutting edge of middle-class trendiness, yet they kept telling me — not directly and honestly like their beloved working-class would — but subtly and snidely, that if I was a *real* writer I'd be tackling the problems of the real people in our society. The poor, the maimed, the halt and the blind. I must never, never write about the lifestyles *they* themselves were leading. *Pricks!* Loathsome, do gooding, trendy pricks! Stuff them!

KATE: Perhaps they felt it was a little self-indulgent to concentrate on the the problems of the middle-class when the problems of the disadvantaged are so much more acute.

COLIN: I see. The middle-class have no *real* problems. So how is it they manage to pack so many traumas and breakdowns into their sunny middle-class lives? How is it that they unerringly turn every relationship they embark on into the storyline of a soap opera?

KATE: I don't think that comment's justified Colin. Teresa's been married for eighteen years.

COLIN: Yes, but has anyone ever *seen* Gavin in the last fifteen? I know he's supposed to be writing poetry upstairs, but my guess is that he's been in Katmandu since the early seventies.

KATE: [*finding his histrionics amusing*] Colin.

COLIN: I know the middle-class shouldn't have emotional problems — they're infinitely better off in a material sense than your average third world villager — but for some perverse reason they successfully screw up their lives with great flair, and I find that interesting, and I'm going to keep charting their perturbations and try and make some sense of it all, and those Chardonnay socialists of Melbourne aren't going to stop me!

KATE: [*to the audience*] If I hated Sydney that much, why did I agree to come? In hindsight I suspect that there was something in me that responded to that odd, pulsing, garish city to the north. A reckless streak, a habit of getting quickly bored — I think that deep down I felt something might *happen* up here. And until it did I was in the happy position of having Colin to blame for all the misfortunes that befell us.

COLIN: [*to the audience*] I shouldn't've been so bloody reckless. What kind of idiot uproots himself from a lifetime of connections for childhood memories of flame trees and jacarandas? Lunatic. But *was* it just that? Wasn't there a little grub in my soul hungry for the lionising and celebrity mania that grips the harbour city? Devouring my integrity until I drifted towards the sun and journalists who asked me what I'd like to see in my Christmas stocking and did I sleep nude?

> [KATE *exits*. COLIN *stands by himself. We hear the noise of cocktail party chatter.* MIKE McCORD *approaches him.* MIKE *is a smartly-dressed man about the same age as* COLIN. *His hair is carefully swept up over his brow in a stylish sweep. His manner is abrupt, authoritative and conspiratorial, conveying the impression that he knows far more than anybody about everything.*]

MIKE: Colin Rogers?
COLIN: [*awkwardly*] That's right.
MIKE: Mike McCord. Welcome to Sydney.
COLIN: Thanks.
MIKE: Seen any of his films?
COLIN: [*not understanding*] Sorry?
MIKE: [*inclining his head*] Our guest. The Hun.
COLIN: No.
MIKE: Don't rush. Best he's ever done is win a jury prize at the Dublin film festival, which places his talent pretty exactly.

> [COLIN *smiles and shakes his head.*]

COLIN: Dublin.
MIKE: None of his films have ever made a cent, so what does our Film Commission do? Throws a cocktail party for him.
COLIN: I don't usually go to these things. Hate 'em.
MIKE: Go to all the cocktail parties. Golden rule of Sydney life. Only time you ever learn anything. There are the McElroy brothers over there. Only non-identical twins you

can't tell apart. Saw one of your old movies on video last weekend.

COLIN: [*steeling himself against possible criticism*] Ah. Which one?

MIKE: *Days of Wine and Whitlam.*

COLIN: Ah.

MIKE: Enjoyed it. Can't work out why the critics were so savage.

COLIN: [*tense*] Most of the crits were very good.

MIKE: [*shrugging*] Must have read one of the bad ones. No, I enjoyed it. Good entertainment.

COLIN: [*bristling*] A little more than that, I hope.

MIKE: End was a bit of a worry. I would've been inclined to tie up the loose ends.

COLIN: [*curtly*] Loose ends were symptomatic of the times. You write yourself do you?

MIKE: Got some projects on the boil. Yep.

COLIN: What sort of projects?

MIKE: Contemporary action-adventure. Right for today's market.

COLIN: [*tight lipped*] That's what we all should be writing then is it? Contemporary action-adventure.

[MIKE *misses the sarcasm.*]

MIKE: [*nodding*] Look around you. Yesterday's men. Cranking out pictures that nobody wants to see any more. Slow pans over the vast outback. Pretty pictures. No action. No drama. It's about time we woke up to the fact that the little bit of history we've had has been so bloody dull there's no point trying to mythologise it. We've got to start making films that are hard-hitting, contemporary and international. Movies that'll work all over the world. What are you working on?

COLIN: [*reluctantly*] Another script.

MIKE: Is it going to be contemporary?

COLIN: Recent history.

MIKE: Given up on the middle-classes?

COLIN: [*defensively*] I feel like a change.

MIKE: Elaine Ross producing?

COLIN: I imagine so.

MIKE: Haven't asked her yet?

COLIN: Not yet. No.

MIKE: Ever thought of producing your own scripts?

COLIN: It's hard enough to write them.

MIKE: Worth considering. More money, greater artistic control.

COLIN: Elaine's always done my scripts well.

> [MIKE *rocks his head backwards and forwards, indicating that he's not sure he agrees.*]
> You don't think so?

MIKE: If you're happy, fine. Got a project I'd like to talk to you about. Got an hour or so next week?

COLIN: [*to the audience*] What I should have said was, '*No*'. Not this week, next week or any other week. The man was patently a hustler and a spectacularly insensitive human being. It was the confidence and assurance that made me hesitate. In my defence it's an industry in which today's joke is tomorrow's genius. Lucas, Spielberg — laughed at by the studios when they first did the rounds. Who knows where the next hot project is going to emerge from? And it was only a few minutes of my time. [*To* MIKE] Sure.

MIKE: [*fishing for a notebook*] I'll get your number.

> [MIKE *takes the number and exits.* COLIN *stands staring ahead, deep in thought.* KATE *enters.*]

KATE: How was the cocktail party?

COLIN: Appalling. Last time I go to one of those. Everyone in the room knew who I was, but not *one* of them came across to say, 'hello'. I don't expect anyone to genuflect, but I do happen to be the screenwriter with the best track record in the country and not one of them came and said, 'hello'.

KATE: You can look a bit . . . unapproachable. Why didn't you walk up and introduce yourself?

COLIN: I hate *imposing* myself. I hate the humiliation of having to *loom*.

> [COLIN *acts himself looming.* KATE *smiles.*]

Standing there with your facial muscles going rigid around a forced smile, blood freezing in your veins as you wait at the edge of a conversation for the circle to widen — until finally you croak, 'Mind if I join you', and everybody looks at you as if you'd just farted. Why are Australian's so bloody graceless? Why can't we *occasionally* show a little social tact and flair?

KATE: You're too sensitive, Colin. A dozen people probably wanted to talk to you, but were just as nervous about approaching you as you were about them.

COLIN: [*gloomily*] If you do make the effort and approach someone, it inevitably turns out to be the most boring person in the room, and you're stuck. If you leave too soon they'll know you think they're boring, and if you stay, they catch you glancing desperately over their shoulder and say, 'I'm boring you aren't I?'', and you shriek 'No!'', and you're stuck for another hour. I find mass social intercourse a total mystery. Nobody likes it but it keeps on happening.

KATE: [*smiling*] Colin, you're so *inept*. All you've got to do is say, 'Ah, there's Dennis: catch up with you later.' Being scrupulously polite to all people at all times makes you just as many enemies as being rude.

COLIN: The only guy that did come and talk to me was some aging shyster who script edits soap operas.

KATE: What did he want?

COLIN: He's trying to get a project up.

KATE: And he wants you to write it?

COLIN: I expect so.

KATE: You're not going to talk to him about it?

COLIN: Won't do any harm. There's just an odd chance it might be brilliant.

KATE: [*reprovingly*] Colin!

COLIN: [*irritated*] There's no harm in *talking* to the man. Don't you think I can look after myself?

KATE: [*to the audience*] Frankly, no. Colin does his best to appear confident, but just under that prickly surface is a monumental insecurity and an almost childlike desire to please. If I hadn't been round to rescue him from the hucksters and operators, his career up to now would've been a disaster.

[*They exit.* MIKE McCORD *enters with his girlfriend* HELEN. *She's a lot younger than he and is smart, engaging, buoyant and very sexy.*]

MIKE: Met Colin Rogers today.

HELEN: [*impressed*] Really?

MIKE: Had a long chat.

HELEN: Where'd you meet him?

MIKE: Film Commission.

HELEN: Did you just walk up to him?

MIKE: What am I supposed to do? Crawl on my hands and knees?

HELEN: [*shrugging*] I would've been a bit nervous.

MIKE: He's just a working writer like I am.

HELEN: You haven't had eight of your screenplays shot.

MIKE: His era's over. The public wants *excitement* when they go to the cinema. Action, adventure — not a bunch of middle-class wankers chatting about their problems.

HELEN: Hate action flicks.

MIKE: Hate action flicks? Cinema *is* action.

HELEN: I occasionally like to exercise my mind.

MIKE: You want to exercise your mind — go and read philosophy. [*To the audience*] Apart from a tendency to worship anything that smelt of culture with a capital 'C', who could fault her? I still look at her and can't believe it's me who gets into bed with her every night. I get erections when I hear her on the phone. I watch her talking to other men and wonder how they can keep their hands off her. And she's funny. And she's smart. And when we screw she goes 'Mmm, Mmm, Mmm,' like she's eating zabaglione, and when she comes she shakes like a jet hitting turbulence.

[MIKE *pauses slightly and gives a worried frown.*]

I'm not putting this all that sensitively. What I'm trying to say is that if what I feel for her isn't love, then it's pretty bloody close.

HELEN: What was he like?

MIKE: Boring.

HELEN: I'd like to meet him.

MIKE: He's boring.

HELEN: I'd still like to meet him.

MIKE: [*shaking his head in disgust*] The power of the media. Just because you've read in some women's magazine that he sleeps in red pyjamas —

HELEN: [*interrupting*] In the nude. He sleeps in the nude.

MIKE: So do I, but it never seems to get you excited.

HELEN: You're not famous.

MIKE: I'll be more famous one day than he is.

HELEN: You get famous, I'll get excited.

MIKE: People come from nowhere in this industry. You can make it on the basis of a three line synopsis written on the back of a coffee chit.

HELEN: [*mischievously rather than cuttingly*] If that's all it takes, why has it taken you so long?

MIKE: Because everyone wants tomorrow's projects, but they won't look at anything unless it's got one of yesterday's names attached.

[MIKE *stares across at* COLIN *as he walks onstage. The name from yesterday he intends to attach. He leaves the stage with* HELEN *as* COLIN *paces up and down waiting for the phone to ring.*]

COLIN: [*to the audience*] I gave Elaine the best outline I'd ever written. Three weeks later she still hadn't phoned. For the first week I put it down to the fact that her five-hour lunches didn't leave her with much time, or in any condition to absorb new material. The sheer rudeness of her silence was unforgivable.

[COLIN *paces up and down, makes a decision, reaches for his coat and storms out the door. He arrives at* ELAINE*'s office. He appears outwardly calm but clenches his right fist and taps his right foot, his characteristic sign that he's distressed.* ELAINE *looks up.*]

ELAINE: Colin.

COLIN: Just passing by. Thought I'd drop in and say hello.

ELAINE: How nice.

[*She knows what he's here for, but pretends she doesn't. There's an awkward pause.*]

COLIN: Busy?

ELAINE: Yes, I am.

COLIN: Money'll be hard to find this year.

ELAINE: Good projects always find their money.

[ELAINE *wants to avoid discussing the outline. She tries to look as if she's desperate to start work again, but* COLIN *stands there shuffling, clenching and looking agitated and uncomfortable.*]

ELAINE: [*with noticeable reluctance*] Would you like some coffee?

COLIN: No, I'd better go.

> [*He's extremely reluctant to go, but having said it he has to finally turn and make for the door. He summons up his courage and turns back.*]

[*Tensely*] Oh, by the way. Did you get a chance to glance at my outline?

ELAINE: Your outline. Yes. Just a quick glance.

COLIN: [*quickly*] It's very rough.

ELAINE: [*nodding*] It's interesting. I was expecting something contemporary.

COLIN: [*quickly*] Were you? Why was that?

ELAINE: Everything else you've done has been contemporary, so I didn't think the assumption was unreasonable.

COLIN: I wanted to move away from contemporary. People have been suggesting that it's all I can do.

ELAINE: What people?

COLIN: Critics, friends.

ELAINE: *Never* let critics force you into areas you don't want to go.

COLIN: I did want to go. It's a story that's important to me.

ELAINE: Coastwatchers?

COLIN: My uncle was one during the war.

ELAINE: My Aunt wrapped red cross parcels, but cinema hasn't suffered irreparably because her story remains untold.

COLIN: [*upset*] They were incredibly brave. They saved this country from invasion.

ELAINE: Do you think it'll have wide appeal?

COLIN: Absolutely.

ELAINE: [*with a false smile*] Let's have lunch next week and talk about it.

COLIN: You don't think it'll have wide appeal?

ELAINE: Let's have lunch and talk about it next week.

COLIN: [*in an impassioned outburst*] Elaine, these men were incredibly brave. Didn't you feel at least slightly moved by what you read in that outline? When's the last time you saw anyone in today's society risking their lives for their fellow countrymen. These men were heroes. Old fashioned, genuine heroes. Can't we make films about heroes any more?

[*The phone rings.* ELAINE *looks immensely grateful. She picks it up, puts her hand over the mouthpiece and turns to him.*]

ELAINE: I'll read it again and ring you.

[ELAINE *turns her attention to the phone.*]

Ross productions. Carmel. I'm so sorry, I've been meaning to call.

[COLIN *clenches his fist. Now he's finally burst forth he wants to continue the debate, but as he watches* ELAINE *nod and smile into the phone, he realises he's not going to have a chance. He turns and leaves.* MIKE *walks onstage.* COLIN *picks up an outline and reads to himself.*]

MIKE: [*addressing the audience*] I had to pitch and hook him. No second chance. Deep down I knew he was yesterday's man and I was the future, but not so deep down, all that media hype about him over the years impressed me against my will. He was such an arrogant prick he'd make anyone nervous. He stood staring at me as if I'm a wood grub and he's a red gum. I took three indigestion tablets and it still didn't stop the flames in my gullet and the fire in my gut. I remember thinking as I swallowed them, 'Why are you doing this? What are you trying to prove?' I knew the answer before I'd finished asking the question. I was trying to prove to every bastard who's ever laughed at me behind my back, sneered at the mention of my name, or sacked me, that despite a less than glorious career in insurance, real estate, sales, advertising, burglar alarms and pigs, I was a top talent waiting for the right time and the right game and I'd found it. And every time I thought of Helen, it made me even more desperate to succeed. I won her on a promise of future greatness and time was running out. I couldn't exist without her. No way. So there I was, wood grub to the red gum, needing him to say, 'yes', because none of those miserable merchant bankers are ever going to trust a script with my name on the front even if they love it, their wives love it, their secretaries love it and it gives off the odour of dollars. With Colin Rogers name on it, my career is launched.

[MIKE *turns to* COLIN. COLIN *puts down the outline of* MIKE*'s and regards him with bemused disdain. Not quite red gum to* *the wood grub, but* COLIN*'s manner does indicate that he feels comfortably superior to him.*]

COLIN: Certainly full of action.

MIKE: Based on fact.

COLIN: Really?

MIKE: Absolutely.

COLIN: Shoot-outs?

MIKE: Anything goes up in the gulf. It's like the wild west.

COLIN: Next time I eat a prawn I'll appreciate the drama behind it.

MIKE: Structure's neat. Notice how when the seventeen year old spunk is hired as cook, she focusses all the tensions?

COLIN: Yes. What are you going to call it? *Prawn Wars?*

MIKE: [*with a forced laugh*] *Night Boats.*

COLIN: *Night Boats.*

MIKE: Nothing's set in concrete. The girl doesn't have to be swallowed by the crocodile.

COLIN: Saves her having to choose between the men.

MIKE: How do you feel about the overall concept?

COLIN: Sounds highly commercial.

MIKE: Absolutely. Would you like to co-write it? You'd get first credit of course, and we'd produce it ourselves so that we make some money, and keep control. No slow pans over gulf sunsets, and no Jack Thompson and Bryan Brown. The only bit of decent casting in an Australian movie was the horse in Phar Lap.

COLIN: [*bristling*] I think the casting in my movies has been quite good.

MIKE: Who thought of Stewart Egan as the lead in *Days of Wine and Whitlam?*

COLIN: Elaine Ross.

MIKE: [*nodding knowingly*] Stewart Egan looks O.K. on rock clips, but he was a disaster on film.

COLIN: [*coldly*] I didn't think he was bad.

MIKE: Producers who cast *names* instead of good *actors* and think it'll earn them megabucks, don't know the business they're in. Egan might've been a big rock star, but the public know he can't *act*, so they stayed away in droves.

COLIN: [*coldly*] Stayed away in droves?

MIKE: I know it made it's money back.

COLIN: It made a healthy profit.

MIKE: It could've made a *massive* profit. It was a great screenplay. Didn't it win the best screenplay at ...

COLIN: Berlin.

MIKE: [*nodding*] Not best actor. Not best director. Best screenplay. One of the best that's ever been written in this country, but the public stayed away in droves because Elaine Knucklehead Ross cast a lead actor who'd make your average corpse look as if it was tap dancing. And why the hell did she let Scranton direct it?

COLIN: [*defensively*] He's not my favourite director but he did a competent enough job.

MIKE: Scranton can barely direct shit from his arsehole. Your script *made* him, if you call success screwing up historical epics in Hollywood. Your scripts have *made* Elaine Ross too.

COLIN: I wouldn't say that.

MIKE: She's the one living in splendour in Darling Point. You're stuck here in a terrace in Paddington. Why should she have the harbour views? You're the one with the talent. *Night Boats*. What do you think?

COLIN: I'm not sure it's my type of project.

MIKE: I don't need an answer straight away. Sleep on it. It's got colour, action, tension, pathos, romance. What were you working on again? Recent history wasn't it?

COLIN: Yes.

MIKE: Second World War?

COLIN: [*looking up sharply*] Why?

MIKE: You know Gary McBride at Channel Ten?

COLIN: No.

MIKE: Gary's a mate of mine. Says Second World War always rates. What angle are you taking?

COLIN: [*reluctantly*] Coastwatchers.

MIKE: Coastwatchers?

COLIN: The men who stayed behind on Jap occupied islands and reported Jap ship movements by radio. They saved us from a full-scale invasion.

MIKE: We could get this one up mate. Gary said that if I ever had anything second world war to come straight to him.

COLIN: I'm developing it for film.

MIKE: [*shaking his head*] Second World War doesn't rate on the big screen, mate. This is television. Six hour, eight hour mini-series. I could get a pre sale from Gary within a week, go straight to a merchant bank for underwriting, and we'd be shooting by August.

COLIN: I'd rather see it as a movie.

MIKE: It's an epic story, mate. How could you tell it in two hours?

> [MIKE *exits.* COLIN *crosses to discuss his future with* ELAINE.]

ELAINE: Television?

COLIN: A six-hour or eight-hour mini-series.

ELAINE: Colin, I know how passionate you are about this, and I truly want to believe, but I keep on stumbling over the fact that Coastwatchers basically watched coasts. I can't see eight hours of television.

COLIN: [*passionately*] They fought guerilla actions, they were always on the run — they ran incredible risks! My uncle used to tell me the stories when I was a kid.

ELAINE: Colin, the impact an uncle can have on a young kid is one thing. If we go the television route I've got to sell the concept to network executives with sloping foreheads and neanderthal brows who are living proof that we share ninety-nine percent of our D.N.A. with the higher apes, and they only ever ask one question: 'Why in the hell would Mr and Mrs Western Suburbs want to watch that shit?' Which is an odd question when the opposition channel is featuring a wrestling bout between King Kong Bundy and Junkyard Dog, but they still ask it.

COLIN: Surely you can sell them quality occasionally?

ELAINE: There are executives in our networks, who, if asked to name an American intellectual would answer, 'Sylvester Stallone'. Colin, if you want to go in a new direction, I've got the perfect project for you. Have you heard the name Tony Sanzari?

COLIN: Yes, but I can't remember the context.

ELAINE: He's the father of the two boys killed in that fun park accident.

> [COLIN *nods without enthusisam.*]

COLIN: Ah. Yes.

ELAINE: He's waged an incredible one man war against the authorities to prove it wasn't an accident.

COLIN: [*bored*] He's a bit of a nut case, isn't he?

ELAINE: [*quietly angry*] I think he's anything but a nut case. He's got very convincing proof that the so called 'accident' was organised by one of the country's biggest crims so he could get the park condemned and buy it up cheap for development. And there've been two serious attempts on his life while he was getting that proof.

COLIN: If he's got proof, why don't the authorities do something?

ELAINE: Because a lot of money has been spread around to make sure that they don't.

COLIN: I can't get excited by corruption, Elaine, it's so bloody sordid.

ELAINE: Can you get excited by the story of a father who's so shattered by the loss of his sons that he'd risk his own life to get the man responsible? You've got kids. Imagine how you'd feel?

COLIN: Elaine!

ELAINE: [*with a tough glint in her eye*] It's a powerful story and it should be told and I want you to tell it.

COLIN: I'm sorry. It doesn't appeal.

ELAINE: Colin, I've paid a fortune for the rights.

COLIN: I want to do *Coastwatchers*.

ELAINE: *Coastwatchers* is a turkey!

COLIN: [*angrily*] How can you say that? It hasn't been written yet!

ELAINE: Colin, it's a turkey!

COLIN: All right. I'll do it myself.

ELAINE: Produce it?

COLIN: Yes!

ELAINE: Don't be ridiculous, Colin. What experience have you ever had in production?

COLIN: It's about time I learned.

ELAINE: Have you any idea what's involved?

COLIN: Nothing that any intelligent person couldn't handle.

ELAINE: Is that so?

COLIN: It's time I started taking more responsibility for the key creative decisions.

ELAINE: Are there any creative decisions *I've* taken that you've been unhappy with?

COLIN: [*averting his eyes*] One or two.

ELAINE: Which ones?

COLIN: Casting Stewart Egan in *Days of Wine and Whitlam.*

ELAINE: [*incensed*] Egan was wonderful.

COLIN: I felt he was wooden.

ELAINE: Wooden?

COLIN: Mahogony, Teak. Possibly even Jarrah.

ELAINE: I'm sorry you didn't mention your doubts about him when I showed you the screen tests — you didn't seem to have any of these polished wood anxieties then. In fact you told me he was the only possible choice.

COLIN: [*averting his eyes*] I didn't want to rock the boat.

ELAINE: You told me you couldn't believe it was the same man who did the rock clips.

COLIN: [*embarrassed*] I can't remember saying that.

ELAINE: You did.

COLIN: Everybody gets a bit over-optimistic when a film is coming together.

ELAINE: [*coldly furious*] Are there any other mistakes you think I've made?

COLIN: [*backing off*] This isn't the time to nit-pick over old grievances.

ELAINE: What are the others?

COLIN: I don't think this is the time —

ELAINE: [*interrutping*] Richard Scranton as director? I suppose I made a mistake there too?

COLIN: I wasn't entirely happy —

ELAINE: [*interrupting*] I don't believe it. The man is now a top Hollywood talent. Has Hollywood been over here begging you to get on the plane?

COLIN: [*stung*] If I was prepared to write mindless genre pieces they probably would be.

ELAINE: [*with Arctic coldness*] I'm sorry you won't do the Sanzari story Colin. I think it's going to make the writer who does do it very famous.

COLIN: [*to the audience*] That's a threat that chills any writer
to the marrow of their bones. A dozen other writers I'd
hate to see collecting a bronze statuette flashed before my
eyes, but for once in my life I stuck to my guns. Why was
I so obsessed with *Coastwatchers*? Dogged loyalty to the
memory of Uncle Jimmy. I was a lonely kid whose own
parents devoted all their energies to bitter marital warfare,
and Jimmy, whose own marriage had been a childless
disaster, made me the son he was never going to have. I
idolised him. His coastwatcher stories became sagas of
infinite importance to me, and I questioned him about every
rock, every tree, every close encounter, and every death.
I wanted answers to the most urgent, chilling and unsettling
questions in my young mind. How does one face death,
and how can one man kill another? Jimmy told me
something he'd never told anyone else. He'd killed a
Japanese soldier who'd come to the edge of a clearing in
the moonlight. At first he couldn't shoot, then the soldier
began to urinate and Jimmy felt a wave of disgust and
pulled the trigger and had had nightmares ever since. How
could he kill a man for urinating in the open when he
himself had done it half an hour before? *Coastwatchers* had
to answer that question. It was a shrine I was building to
the memory of Uncle Jimmy.
    [MIKE *enters.*]
MIKE: [*to the audience*] *Coastwatchers*? I hated every minute of
it, but the writing was the worst. The status difference
between us stood out like a hooker in the lobby of the Hyatt
Hilton. I sat there, grublike, over the typewriter while Red
Gum strode up and down dictating the thing word for word.
When I got so pissed off I couldn't stand it any longer I'd
throw in a suggestion and there'd be a frozen silence and
he'd look up at the ceiling and say, [*imitating* COLIN]
'Nooo, I don't think so.' Then he'd stare at me. We'd
eyeball to eyeball for about a sixteenth of a second and I'd
go back to my typing. And the subject? *Coastwatchers*, quite
frankly, interested me about as much as going to bed with
a six-foot, fourteen-stone lesbian, which I have done under
odd circumstances I won't bore you with. But an odd thing
happened. I started reading the words I was typing out of

sheer boredom, and found that this arrogant prick, striding up and down like Napoleon plus growth hormones, was telling a story that was getting me in. Guys taking incredible risks under appalling conditions so that fat little babies like myself slept on undisturbed. In the world I see around me where everyone is out for number one, this sort of behaviour gives you an odd jolt. The turd had the odd knack of making his characters live. He didn't have my visual sense, though, and towards the end I started sneaking in some of my images.

[MIKE *exits.* COLIN *strides up and down the room gesticulating. He's acting out some of the crucial scenes he's about to write the next day. He doesn't speak the lines out loud but emits a curious, high speed mumble, rather like a tape recorder being played backwards at triple speed.* KATE *watches him. She's used to it, but is still irritated by his total absorption in his work.*]

KATE: Penny lied about where she was last weekend.

COLIN: Penny? She's never lied in her life.

KATE: Well, she's just started.

COLIN: Wasn't she here last weekend?

KATE: Colin, as a father you're a joke.

COLIN: As a wife you don't give me many laughs.

KATE: If you ever give another interview in which you claim to do fifty percent of the household chores and put the reponsibilities of fatherhood before your work I'll ring the bloody journalist and demand the right of reply.

COLIN: I do the shopping.

KATE: I pin a series of lists headed 'butcher', 'greengrocer', 'delicatessen' to your jumper which you usually manage to leave at the right shop and which you often remember to collect. I'm the one who does all the thinking.

COLIN: *I'll* do the thinking, *you* spend an hour a day behaving like a fork lift truck. Have you ever had to have a prolonged conversation with Doug the butcher? He's a great guy, but after the weather it can get tricky. Especially when the only reason he can think of as to why I do the shopping at ten every morning and why I don't speak like an outback Queenslander, is that I'm the boyfriend of a Qantas flight director.

KATE: Let him think it.

COLIN: I don't want him to think it. I'm not.

KATE: There's nothing wrong with being gay.

COLIN: Nothing wrong at all, except that I'm not. And while we're on this, will you stop all this nauseating stuff with young Sam about, 'No one knows what one's sexual preferences will be until one grows up, but if one's sexual preferences *do* turn out to be minority preferences, one must *never* be ashamed of it.'

KATE: You're just prejudiced against gays.

COLIN: I am not in the *least* prejudiced against gays. I just want the kid not to feel guilty if by some odd chance he grows up hetero.

KATE: You *are* prejudiced.

COLIN: It took fifteen million years of evolution for my genes to get to me, I'd just like to see them go a bit further. Where *was* Penny?

KATE: At a disco called 'Downmarket'. She was supposed to be studying at her friend's place.

COLIN: Disco? When she was in Melbourne the only thing she'd listen to was Mozart.

KATE: I'd be surprised if 'Downmarket' is noted for its Mozart.

COLIN: How did you find out?

KATE: A twenty-three-year-old German tourist turned up on our doorstep looking for our daughter.

COLIN: What did he want?

KATE: It wasn't Mozart. Apparently he felt an offer had been made on the dance floor.

COLIN: [*shocked*] That's terrible. She's only thirteen.

KATE: Fifteen, but it's still a worry.

COLIN: Those disco's are where the pushers operate.

KATE: Our daughter says it isn't a problem. If you stay out on the dance floor they soon stop bothering you.

COLIN: We'll have to do something.

KATE: I've stopped this week's pocket money.

COLIN: [*agitated*] That'll really strike terror into her.

KATE: What do you want me to do? Lock her in a dark cupboard for a month?

COLIN: This is serious. She's rubbing shoulders — and God

knows what else — with pushers and pimps. What's made her interested in disco's, for God's sake?

KATE: This is a very cosmopolitan city.

COLIN: Disco's aren't cosmopolitan, they're tawdry.

KATE: I was going to say tawdry, but I didn't want to be rude about your chosen city.

COLIN: Don't sit there being smug. This is serious. We've got to take firm action.

KATE: What do you suggest?

COLIN: If we let her keep on going like this she'll end up in William street hopping into passing Jaguars.

KATE: If you're so worried, you take over the problem. And you can handle Sam and Hannah as well.

COLIN: What's wrong with Sam and Hannah?

KATE: Sam's apparently running a protection racket in his sixth grade —

COLIN: [interrupting] Protection racket? In Melbourne we couldn't get him away from his computer.

KATE: New city, new skills. And Hannah's teachers say she's depressed.

COLIN: Who wouldn't be in this family?

KATE: How about taking some of the blame for that yourself? You can go to the schools and hear the bad news next time! I'm sick to death of organising this menagerie. I've got problems of my own.

COLIN: Such as?

KATE: Such as going quietly crazy because my idiot boss refuses to publish the first manuscript in years that's got me excited.

COLIN: That black woman's novel?

KATE: I wish you wouldn't keep calling her, 'that black woman.'

COLIN: What am I expected to call her? 'That woman whose complexion is not as ours?'

KATE: Call her by her *name*.

COLIN: I forget it.

KATE: Take the trouble to *learn*. You've heard it often enough. Her name is Kath Mitchell and her book is called —

COLIN: [*interrupting*] I know the name of her book. Who could forget it? 'Black Rage.'

KATE: See?

COLIN: See what?

KATE: The tone of contempt.

COLIN: It's a terrible title.

KATE: Just because she's a member of a minority who've been made marginal in a land they owned for forty thousand years, and a member of another minority who've been made marginal by the post agricultural patriachy for eight thousand years, doesn't entitle you to dismiss *her* or her *work*.

COLIN: I haven't.

KATE: You'd better not. It gives her work a lot of power.

COLIN: Whereas mine, being pale and male, is limp?

KATE: You're work hasn't got her power. No.

COLIN: [*hurt*] Thank you.

KATE: [*attempting tact, which she's not very good at*] But yours has got certain qualities hers hasn't.

COLIN: Of course. It's more frivolous, less passionate, less committed. You know, I've got a certain sympathy for your boss. Why *shouldn't* he publish stuff people want to read, instead of yet another frothing-mouthed cry of rage from yet another disadvantaged minority? I *hated* those bleak Melbourne bookshops full of surly pinched-faced zealots shuffling down corridors stacked with envy, anger and hate.

KATE: You prefer Sydney bookshops? Filled with cookbooks?

COLIN: If people want cookbooks, let them have cookbooks.

KATE: I'm not devoting my life to improving the North shore souffle!

COLIN: Of course not. You're going to keep trying to publish stuff that nobody wants to read.

KATE: I'm going to keep trying to publish books which prick the consciences of a few thousand people out there and make them aware that under the gloss of affluence there is *real* suffering. Did you know that rents are so high in this sub-tropical lotus land that all the women's hostels are overflowing and five hundred women and their kids are being turned away every week? Families are out there sleeping on golf courses and in car wrecks?

COLIN: What do you want me to do? Go to my nearest golf course and redirect them here? What do your two thousand pricked consciences actually go and *do* when they've put down the book?

KATE: Eventually they change the consciousness of this nation. They make it a fairer place for everyone.

COLIN: Kate, the country isn't going to become fair because someone in a book says it should be. The unpalatable truth is that we're an egocentric species who care a lot about ourselves and our children, a little bit for our tribe, and not much at all for anyone else.

KATE: Where did you pick up that right-wing drivel?

COLIN: Kate, can you be honest with yourself for a change without *posing*? Whenever one of those ads comes on urging us to save starving children, we're shocked by the images of the emaciated kids, we look at each other and murmur 'Must do something', but we don't even *note down the number*. But if our young Sam so much as whimpers in the night, we're instantly awake, bolt upright, staring at each other with fear in our eyes. Face up to this awful equation: one cut finger of Sam's equals more anguish than a thousand deaths in Ethiopia!

   [*The logic hits home.*]

KATE: All right. Most of us *are* selfish. We're taught to be.

COLIN: We aren't taught! No parent is *taught* to care more about their child than someone else's!

KATE: All right. We *are* selfish, but we can be taught to change. We can be taught to *care* about others. Sometimes the process is slow and you don't think it's happening at all, but it is. We don't have eight-year-olds working in mine pits any more. Perhaps you hadn't noticed?

COLIN: [*suddenly reflective*] No, we don't.

KATE: Things *can* change for the better, but I'm sure you're not convinced.

COLIN: I want to be convinced. I *hate* the thought that humanity is grasping and egocentric, but the evidence often seems overwhelming, and some of it comes from pretty close to home.

KATE: You mean me?

COLIN: No, I mean *me*.

[*Pause.*]

KATE: I *am* getting tired of organising this family Colin. You're too self-obsessed to ever do your share and I'm starting to feel very, very trapped.

[KATE *exits.*]

COLIN: [*to the audience*] That wasn't exactly music to my ears. I knew the dream behind that threat. A room in Glebe where she'd write short stories for women's anthologies published by McPhee Gribble. And they'd be about leaving a husband who was so thick he had to have shopping lists pinned to his jumpers and so right-wing he voted Labor. If our domestic harmony was precarious, it became even more so after Kate met Mike.

[MIKE *enters the kitchen and reads the morning paper. He's wearing nothing except a towel around his waist.* KATE *enters wearing a dressing-gown and stares at him.*]

KATE: Good morning. I'm Kate.

[MIKE *looks up and then down.*]

MIKE: Hi.

KATE: I was going to pop my head in and say, 'hello' when I got home last night, but I thought I wouldn't interrupt. You, er, stayed overnight?

MIKE: [*not looking up*] Raining. Couldn't get a cab.

KATE: You're both working here again today?

MIKE: [*not looking up*] Going to work here from now on. Much more room.

KATE: Ah.

[KATE *looks at the paper* MIKE *is reading. She has come downstairs to collect it.*]

KATE: Anything interesting?

[MIKE *looks up, puzzled.*]

KATE: Anything interesting happen in the world overnight?

MIKE: [*looking down*] No. Same old shit. Makes you wonder why you keep reading it.

[KATE *hopes this means he'll stop reading it, but it doesn't.*]

KATE: Could you possibly leave the paper there when you've finished? I like to glance at the headlines before the children get up.

MIKE: [*still reading*] Right.

[KATE *gets visibly irritated. She takes an electric jug and plugs it in, banging it down noisily.*]

MIKE: Making coffee?

KATE: Yes.

MIKE: Could you pour me a weak one with no sugar?

KATE: [*tersely*] Are you married, Mike?

MIKE: Have been. Twice.

KATE: But not now?

MIKE: [*still reading*] Right.

[*Pause.*]

Present lady won't marry me.

[KATE*'s look indicates that she finds this far from surprising.*]

MIKE: [*still reading*] *Richard Mahony*'s collapsed.

KATE: Sorry?

MIKE: The movie Tony Klineberg's supposed to be directing. He's talking here as if it's all happening, but the money fell through three days ago.

KATE: Was it a film of the novel?

MIKE: [*nodding*] Thought it would fold.

KATE: Wonderful novel.

MIKE: Screenplay was shithouse. Actor mate of mine got me a copy.

KATE: The novel was wonderful.

MIKE: Screenplay was shithouse. Doctor's marriage goes bad, he goes to the goldfields, gets gangrene and dies. Can't see the crowds queuing in Pitt street for that little number.

KATE: I don't think your synopsis quite does the book justice.

MIKE: [*shrugging*] Screenplay was a real downer.

KATE: What does your friend do?

MIKE: [*looking up, puzzled*] What friend?

KATE: The woman you live with.

MIKE: [*going back to the paper*] Not nearly enough.

KATE: [*getting really irritated*] She's not working?

MIKE: Freelance P.R. Gets about one good job a month and usually stuffs it up.

KATE: Lacks experience?

MIKE: Lacks grey matter.

KATE: Does she mind you having such a low opinion of her?

MIKE: She's got her good points.

KATE: I'm glad to hear it.

MIKE: She's a woman, which is more than you can say for half the dragons around this town.

KATE: What exactly do you mean, Mike — 'She's a woman'?

MIKE: Looks good. Wears nice clothes. Doesn't screech at you like a white cockatoo. Funny. Has the occasional tantrum, and she's so sexy she's dangerous.

KATE: That's your definition of a woman?

MIKE: Yep. And I'm sticking with it.

KATE: Don't you think it's a little bit limited?

MIKE: If some women want to be pile drivers, that's fine. As long as they don't expect me to get under 'em.

[MIKE *exits*. COLIN *enters*. KATE *is not happy*.]

KATE: He's awful! I didn't believe that men like that still existed. What kind of woman would tolerate him?

COLIN: I can't begin to imagine. Some anaemic little scrubber who enjoys being booted around, I suppose.

KATE: Why are you working with the man?

COLIN: I'm going to produce this script myself and I need some help.

KATE: You're letting him *co-write* this script with you? What's he done?

COLIN: He's not co-writing. He's sitting there typing what I tell him.

KATE: His name will be on it as co-writer.

COLIN: [*cutting in*] Everybody's going to know he didn't do anything. All he's done up to now is script edit soapies.

KATE: So why are you working with him?

COLIN: He knows where to look for finance.

KATE: You said you were going to approach Malcolm Bennett. You've known Malcolm for years.

COLIN: [*uneasy*] Mike gave me the confidence to realise I could produce my own scripts.

KATE: You've never had any complaints about Elaine up to now.

COLIN: Elaine *hated* this idea. Right?

KATE: She still would have done it.

COLIN: I don't want to work with someone who doesn't believe in what I'm doing. She can find someone else to make her rich.

KATE: Make her rich?

COLIN: Who's got that stunning harbour view? She has. Not me.

KATE: This city's getting to you already.

COLIN: I wouldn't mind a nice view. Is that so decadent?

KATE: You're working with Mike so you can buy yourself a nice view?

COLIN: [*tensely*] I am perfectly aware of the fact that Mike is a buffoon, but he obeys orders, does what he's told and he's helping me get what I want.

KATE:[*nodding*] A stunning harbour view.

COLIN: Creative control! Deciding who's cast. Deciding who directs. Making sure the script is shot as I wrote it. And if there *is* some money to be made, making sure I'm the one who gets it.

KATE: He's using you, Colin. Getting co-authorship of one of your scripts means he's going from nothing to something in one huge jump.

COLIN: Everyone in the business will know I wrote it all.

KATE: You think you're using him, but he's using you.

COLIN: [*irritated*] I can look after myself.

> [KATE *exits.* COLIN *sits in an armchair and thinks.* MIKE *enters and sits poised at the typewriter. Suddenly* COLIN *bounds up out of his chair and starts pacing around waving a clenched fist as if he is threatening the gods of creativity with physical violence if they don't start the ideas flowing.*]

COLIN: The trouble with this scene is that there's nothing at *stake*! Unless something's at stake you have no emotional undercurrent and all you're left with is two people chatting. What's at *stake*?

MIKE: [*dutifully repeating the magic litany*] What's at stake?

COLIN: Hold it a minute while I think this one through.

> [COLIN *returns to his armchair and to deep thought.* MIKE *looks to the heavens as if to say 'How much more of this do I have to put up with?'*]

MIKE: [*to the audience*] I began to think I wasn't going to last the distance. My stomach was giving me hell. Every morning it'd flicker from yesterday's embers and by the end of the day I'd have your full fireball. I was taking three times as many tablets a day as I should've been but it had as much effect as pissing on a bushfire. [*To* COLIN] Just make a quick call.

[MIKE *picks up the phone and dials.*]

MIKE: [*into the phone*] Bob? How about a drink? Six-thirty at the Admiral's Cup bar. Heard about Terry's film? *Disaster.* Absolute disaster. Only took three thousand over the long weekend.

[*He nods.*]

Disaster. See you at six-thirty.

COLIN: Terry's film not doing well?

MIKE: Disaster.

COLIN: Do you know what really amazes me about this industry, Mike? I've got the best track record on script in the country and that phone never rings. Terry could've asked me to write that script and I could've made it work. But he didn't. They never do.

MIKE: [*to the audience*] If I'd've heard him whinge once more about why producers weren't lining up to plead for his services, I'd've perforated. The thing that amazed me about him was that he knew nothing about how the real world operated. The reason producers weren't flocking to him was that they had egos almost as big as his, and who would enjoy crawling on their bellies like I had to do? [*To* COLIN] I'll get some coffee.

[MIKE *leaves.*]

COLIN: [*to the audience*] I watched Mike with the fascination of a zoologist who's found a new species. Port Jackson huckster. He kept ringing around an endless list of contacts, all male, and arranged meetings. The currency being exchanged at the meetings was failure. Other people's. It seemed crucial to Mike that everything failed. If there was a film due for release that seemed in any danger of being declared a success, Mike and his drinking mates would expend enormous amounts of mental energy cracking its pretentions like a walnut. I had an image of Mike as a kind of filmic gridiron player, waiting with the ball until all of his opponents were lying bloody and prostrate so that he could wend his way through them to the touchline. I found this behaviour amusing and reassuring. Other people's failures are always reassuring, but the frantic energy and effort he put into his networking of failure was worrying.

[KATE *comes home looking upset.*]

What's wrong?

KATE: I'm so angry I can't even talk about it. The children are all screaming for food, I suppose?

COLIN: Don't worry about that. We'll phone up for some pizzas. He's not going to publish?

KATE: I just wanted to grab that hollow little man by his collar and hurl him down that sparkling blue harbour he's paid seventy thousand dollars a year to gaze at. I know you can't understand my passion about that book —

COLIN: [*interrupting*] I can. I'm not totally insensitive.

KATE: I was nearly in tears today. I'm going to have to resign.

COLIN: Don't do that. He'll change his mind.

KATE: No, he won't. He's gutless. And he just doesn't care.

[KATE *moves across and flops into a chair. There's a pause.*]

I didn't mean to hurt you about your work. You write beautifully. You can't be expected to write with her power and passion when you've led such a cosseted life.

[*She sees* COLIN*'s look.*]

What's wrong?

COLIN: That's a bit like saying, 'I'm sorry I said you were indescribably ugly. I've just seen your parents and I understand why.'

[MIKE *returns with the coffee.* KATE *sees him, gives a frozen smile, and leaves.*]

MIKE: What's wrong with Kate?

COLIN: Her boss won't let her publish a book she thinks is crucial.

MIKE: Making things a bit difficult domestically?

COLIN: I agree with her. I think it should be published too.

MIKE: What's it about?

COLIN: A black girl trying to break out of the urban poverty cycle.

[COLIN *picks up some pages* MIKE *has typed and walks away from the desk as he scrutinises them.*]

MIKE: What's the name of Kate's boss?

COLIN: Ian Wall. He reckons, 'blacks don't sell books.'
[MIKE *searches through the teledex and locates the name.* COLIN, *engrossed in the script, doesn't notice.*]

MIKE: What's the writer's name?

COLIN: Kathy Mitchell.
[MIKE *starts dialling.* COLIN *barely notices.*]

MIKE: Ian?
[COLIN *looks up, frowning, but still isn't sure what* MIKE'*s doing.*]

MIKE: Ian, there's a rumour going around that you won't publish Kathy's book?
[*Pause.*]
Kathy Mitchell.
[*Pause.*]
Don't worry about who's speaking, mate, just listen to what I'm telling you. A lot of people reckon it's one of the most important books ever written on the black people's problems and they're bloody mad. They've heard the reason you won't print it is that you said, 'Blacks don't sell books' — and they reckon that's a pretty racist statement.
[*Pause.*]
Well, that's how they feel it comes across, and they're so bloody mad that they're going to give you twenty-four hours and then they're going to start putting up tents around your building and calling the media in.
[MIKE *hangs up.*]

COLIN: [*frowning*] Jesus, Mike! What in the hell do you think you're doing?

MIKE: [*reassuringly*] Blow torch to the belly.
[COLIN *looks anything but reassured. He sits there wondering how in the hell he is going to explain this to* KATE. MIKE *exits. Later:* COLIN *still sits in an armchair.* KATE *enters, smiling and excited.*]

KATE: You won't believe what happened.

COLIN: [*tensely)*] What?

KATE: Ian got a call from some black guerilla group who threatened to bomb the building unless he published. Should have seen the panic. It was wonderful.

COLIN: [*worriedly*] Did he call the police?

KATE: God, no. He's *terrified* of bad publicity.

COLIN: He's going to publish?

KATE: [*nodding*] Three thousand copies. What's your news?

COLIN: I forgot the dishwashing powder and the broccoli.

KATE: I'm sorry I've been so rotten lately. I just started feeling that nothing was ever going to go right again.

COLIN: And the dried apricots. They were on the list, but I made that fatal mistake of going straight to the breakfast foods. Even when I was doing it I kept saying to myself, 'Remember the apricots, remember the apricots', but I didn't.

KATE: Stop it. Sorry I've been so down on the kids. When you're having a bad time at work everything can seem pretty black.

COLIN: No, you're quite right. The kids are appalling. I tried to talk to Penny about her disco going and the like, but the look of pity and contempt on her face at my presumption that I might have any wisdom to offer her stopped me right in my tracks.

KATE: Depressing, isn't it?

COLIN: I spend most of my time taking messages from girls with names like Manon, Melissa and Foxglove. They chat on for hours with each other about which boys are likely to be at what bars when, who's been 'dumped' by who and who's therefore available, who got with who at which party and who doesn't know about it yet, and won't there be hell to pay when they do. What does 'getting with' mean?

KATE: Why?

COLIN: Our daughter seems to be one of the most frequent 'getters with' in town.

KATE: It's just petting. Surprising as it may seem, they're all still virgins.

COLIN: They're the most sophisticated bunch of virgins I've ever heard.

KATE: It's all very innocent. Don't get depressed.

COLIN: The only thing I'm depressed about is that it all sounds so bloody interesting. When's the last time we leapt to the phone to hear who had just got with what? We're totally irrelevant to our daughter's life because as far as she's concerned we're middle-aged stodges whose life is effectively over. And maybe she's right. Maybe all the excitement happens upfront.

KATE: You're morbid tonight.

COLIN: Well don't you ever get struck with a sense of *unfairness*? We're supposed to be professionals at the peak of our powers leading highly interesting lives and our daughter is having all the fun!

KATE: [*wistfully*] Yes. We can have sex every night, but she gets ten times the excitement we do thinking about a session of heavy petting with some spotted adolescent.

COLIN: [*hurt*] I didn't realise it was that bad.

KATE: It happens in every marriage.

COLIN: [*defensively*] It's not exactly cosmic for me either. I watched a rerun of Ryan's daugher the other night and had to search my memory to work out what was happening when Sarah Miles got under the stiff-legged Englishman and started making those plaintive little yelps.

KATE:She was acting. I can't.

[KATE *exits*. MIKE *enters and they have a strategy session.*]

COLIN: He's a typical merchant banker. On the one hand he's urbane, arrogant, cynical, vain and ruthlessly determined to screw you for the last quarter of one percent . . .

MIKE: And on the other hand?

COLIN: [*thinking*] I don't think there is another hand.

MIKE: Can't wait to meet him.

COLIN: Are you O.K.?

MIKE: [*swallowing pills*] Stomach's playing up a bit.

COLIN: Don't worry. It's a good project and he'll go for it. Don't show him you're nervous. Speak to him as if he's a drinking mate.

[*As he enters,* COLIN, *and* MIKE *confront* MALCOLM, *an impeccably dressed, urbane, arrogant, cynical and vain merchant banker.* MIKE *is nervous and out of his class.*]

COLIN: Congratulations on your election.

MALCOLM: You read that embarrassing little item did you? I've no idea how the press picked it up.

[*He turns to* MIKE.]

For my sins I was elected President of 'The Friends of the Opera'.

MIKE: Needs all the friends it can get.

MALCOLM: [*generously trying to cover for* MIKE*'s gaffe*] Don't be too harsh. At it's best moments it can be sublime.

MIKE: I could bore people for a fraction of the cost, but every man to his poison.

COLIN: [*trying to recover the situation*] Have you had time to read the script, Malcolm?

MALCOLM: I read the synopsis. Colin, I've got to be honest with you. I don't think it's our sort of project.

COLIN: [*stunned*] How can you say that when you've only read the synopsis?

MALCOLM: Colin, how do you expect me to get my investors excited about men who sat and watched coasts?

COLIN: [*coldly*] If you read the script, I think you'll find they did a lot more than that.

MALCOLM: Colin, I need a concept that's exciting. Exciting enough to hook investors and convince them that the project will sell here and overseas.

COLIN: This *is* exciting. How a handful of men saved Australia!

MALCOLM: Colin, no one under fifty knows Australia was even threatened, and the rest of the world hardly knows Australia exists. Believe me, after spending half my life boarding and leaving international flights I've come to the conclusion that the only thing the nations of the world have in common is a profound indifference to anything that's ever happened here.

COLIN: So you're saying you'll only underwrite projects that have nothing to do with this country or its history?

MALCOLM: I've got to be absolutely honest. I can't even *think* the word '*Coastwatchers*' without yawning.

COLIN: [*angrily, passionately*] This is a *real* story about *real* people who risked their necks for years at a time so that you and I could be here in this room today! You can't dismiss it without reading the script.

MALCOLM: Look, Colin, it could be the best-written script in the world, but unless it smells exciting it's no use to us.

COLIN: Malcolm, all my scripts have made money for you in the past. You owe it to me to *read* it.

MALCOLM: All right, I'll read it.

COLIN: Sit down and read it now.

MALCOLM: Colin, I've got appointments all afternoon.

COLIN: Malcolm, I spent six months of my life writing this. The least you can do is spend two hours reading it!

MALCOLM: I'll read it. I'll read it tonight and phone you in the morning.

[MALCOLM *exits.*]

MIKE: [*to the audience*] Malcolm was right. The only people who would ever find the concept wildly exciting were the surviving coastwatchers, which gave us a guaranteed audience of three, but we finally got the money. It was the only way Malcolm could get Colin off his back.

COLIN: [*to the audience*] The production and shoot were hellish. Mike was useless. He talked big but knew *nothing*. In a single day we lost our director, art director and cinematographer when he insisted that the opening sequence feature a slow-motion close-up of a Causcasian head being severed by a Samurai sword, leaving newly exposed arteries to pump red blood into white titles. We had to get a line producer in to pick up the pieces two days before the cameras rolled. I turned grey, Mike threw up a lot, but finally, miraculously, it was in the can.

MIKE: [*to the audience*] The shoot went well. Our director walked out on us, but it was just as well. He had no visual flair. Colin panicked every time there was the slightest hiccup but I held things together and we finished right on schedule.

COLIN: [*to the audience*] We finished the mix and sent out the tapes to the critics.

MIKE: [*to the audience*] The critics loved it. I knew we had a disaster on our hands. When critics say 'sensitive' and 'lyrical', the public reads 'slow' and 'arty'. Colin ran around with the crits in his hands beaming at everyone. I nodded politely and waited for the ratings.

[KATE *enters and they wait for the ratings at* MIKE*'s place. It's evening and there's been some drinking.* KATE*, in particular, is showing the effects.*]

COLIN: [*tensely*] Ring them again.

MIKE: They said they'd ring as soon as the figures came through.

KATE: I don't know what you're worried about. It was *wonderful*. Everyone in the country would've been watching. I cried.

COLIN: You always cry.

KATE: When that young boy — that *beautiful* young boy — What was his name?

COLIN: Gary Denton.

KATE: *Gary Denton.* Beautiful golden hair. I would like a *very* deep conversation with that young man.

COLIN: He can barely talk.

KATE: When he died, the tears just flowed.
[*She looks around.*]
How long have you had this place, Mike?

MIKE: Too long.

KATE: [*condescending*] It's charming. Little stairways here and little alcoves there. It's remarkable how *little* space you really need. When we were in China we saw whole families of peasants living in a place *half* the size of this, didn't we, Colin? [*Looking up*] I don't know whether khaki's right for the ceiling though.

MIKE: It used to be white, but we left the window open.
[KATE *laughs loudly.*]

KATE: You're very funny, Mike.

COLIN: Helen says I'm a walking joke.

[KATE *laughs loudly. The phone rings.* MIKE *darts across to it. He listens. He nods. His face shows no emotion. He pouts down the phone.*]

MIKE: Thirteen.

COLIN: [*alarmed*] That can't be right. Are you sure they didn't say thirty?

MIKE: Thirteen. Fourteen in Melbourne.

KATE: Thirteen?

COLIN: [*tersely, to* KATE] Thirteen percent of sets tuned to us.

MIKE: Disaster.

COLIN: It has to be wrong. They only sample a few hundred.

MIKE: A few thousand.

COLIN: The promotion was hopeless.

KATE: To hell with the ratings. We all know what gets ratings. Trash.

COLIN: [*irritated*] Kate, in this business if you don't get ratings you're dead. You can't sell your next project.

MIKE: We'll sell it.

KATE: [*to* COLIN] What next project?

COLIN: I don't want to talk about it.

KATE: You said you were going to do the Sanzari film with Elaine.

COLIN: Kate, I've started producing my own work and I'm not about to take three steps back!

KATE: What's this next project?

COLIN: [*gesticulating*] For Christ's sake, we've just had a catastrophic failure. I'm not in the mood to talk about what I might or might not be doing next!

KATE: It's not a failure. It was excellent.

COLIN: Nobody watched!

KATE: What's this next project?

COLIN: Kate, we've just scored a thirteen! I don't want to talk about it.

> [*He turns away.* KATE *glares at him.* MIKE *tries to defuse the tension.*]

MIKE: [*to* KATE] Colin and I have been knocking around some pretty exciting ideas.

KATE: Such as?

COLIN: [*agitated*] I don't want to discuss it. I don't even know if I'll be doing anything at all after this. I might pack the whole game in and go back to teaching!

KATE: [*to* MIKE] Ideas for what? More mini-series?

MIKE: Long running series.

KATE: [*frowning*] What do you mean? Something like *Dallas*?

MIKE: Field's wide open for a big international hit. Could make millions.

KATE: Television series' are trash!

COLIN: It's barely got to discussion stage!

KATE: You're going to spend the rest of your life writing soap opera?

COLIN: Not writing, producing! And it wouldn't be trash!

KATE: Name me the series that isn't.

MIKE: If we get a U.S. sale we could make millions.

KATE: [*to* COLIN] Since when have you been interested in making millions?

COLIN: What's wrong with making money?

KATE: I think it's very sad.

COLIN: What?

KATE: You came to Sydney an artist, and you're turning into a businessman.

COLIN: We just made art and nobody watched.

KATE: I think it's very sad.

COLIN: If being an artist means that you have to starve, then I don't want to be an artist!

[*He walks away and there's an awkward silence.* HELEN *enters the room behind them.*]

HELEN: Hi there. Sorry I'm late.

MIKE: Hi, honey. This is Colin and Kate.

HELEN: Hi. Doesn't exactly seem to be a celebration going on in here. What were the figures?

MIKE: Thirteen.

HELEN: Oh migod. The series wasn't *that* bad?

KATE: [*incensed*] The series was *good*. *Too* good.

HELEN: [*embarrassed*] I meant in commercial terms. It wasn't very commercial.

KATE: Who cares? *I* am publishing a book that will be lucky to sell a few thousand copies, but it's an important and passionate book and its long term influence will be enormous!

HELEN: [*not aggressively*] You're lucky. You still get your weekly pay cheque no matter how many it sells. Mike and Colin only get paid if they get results.

KATE: Colin *has* been getting results. Not enough to make him a millionaire, but until *very* recently he never wanted that. What good is money? What can you do with it? Buy a house with a better view? Go for another trip to Venice?

HELEN: [*without malice*] I'd like to go on my first trip to Venice. I wouldn't say, 'No' to a house with a better view, either. All we see out of our bedroom window is a twenty-foot-high baby wearing Dri Tots.

KATE: [*to the audience*] She was *exactly* what I expected. A carefully packaged and presented material girl of the eighties. A blow-waved, brittle dolly bird. Totally self-obsessed and convinced that the trinkets of affluence were the ultimate prizes of life.

COLIN: [*to the audience*] My first reaction was that this couldn't be right. This vision — this ravishing, mind-scrambling beauty can't belong to Mike. The gods are unjust, but surely not *that* unjust. I flattered myself that I was a progressive male, totally opposed to reducing women to sex objects, but Helen was a walking male fantasy. I focussed all my powers of imagination on what she'd look like without clothes on, felt ashamed of myself, and by way of compensation, fell desperately in love.

KATE: [*to* COLIN] Well, you're going to have to decide.

COLIN: [*snapping out of it*] Decide what?

KATE: Between art and money.

COLIN: Surely they're not always mutually excited — sorry, mutually exclusive. Why did I say excited?

HELEN: [*to the audience*] Because he was. By me. I liked that, and I liked the fact that he was subtle about it too. He didn't stare at my tits as if they were choc chip ice creams like most of them do. I found him very attractive and thought that if I could ever shake myself free of brainless for a weekend or two it could be exciting. I wouldn't've felt the least bit guilty about his wife either. What a dragon. I thought that if that's what Melbourne does to you, thank God I've never been there. [*To* COLIN] Shakespeare.

KATE: Shakespeare what?

HELEN: He was an artist who made money.

KATE: Shakespeare made money? Surely not.

HELEN: He owned five houses. He died a wealthy man.

MIKE: [*to the audience*] The only trouble with that broad of mine is that she never knows when to shut up. That bloody wife of Colin's was going to put the hard word on Colin to ditch me as soon as possible and Helen makes the situation worse by starting to pick a fight. After putting all that hard slog into the *Coastwatcher* fiasco, there was no way I was going to let go until we got ourselves a smash hit. After that he could write art until his balls dropped off.

KATE: If Shakespeare were alive today, I'm sure he wouldn't be writing *Dallas*.

[MIKE *goes into contortions and belches.*]
    Is something wrong?

MIKE: Stomach's playing up again.

COLIN: We'd better go.

MIKE: Sorry about this. Like a tame tiger snake. Never know when it's going to strike.

COLIN: Thanks for your hospitality.

MIKE: Only wish the news had've been better.

HELEN: Bye, Kate. Bye, Colin.

COLIN: [*to the audience*] I felt the deft touch of her fingers and the breath of her voice in my ear. I felt chemistry between us that would make Sarah Miles and her stiff-legged lover look jaded.

> [MIKE *and* HELEN *exit.* COLIN *and* KATE *stand outside the house.* COLIN *tries to hail a cab.*]

KATE: I hope I never have to meet those two socially again.

COLIN: They're not that bad.

> [COLIN *looks at* KATE, *grits his teeth, misses another taxi and stares straight ahead.*]

KATE: Colin, I'm shocked. Really shocked.

COLIN: [*truculently*] At what?

KATE: I'm shocked that you're going into a continuing relationship with that man and talking seriously about producing soap opera.

COLIN: We're not going to produce soap opera.

KATE: Colin, what's happening to you?

COLIN: [*suddenly, passionately*] What's happening is that I'm getting older and I'm starting to have the nightmare that every writer gets: ending my life as a deadbeat, flogging scripts to producers who don't want 'em. And it's not paranoia. It happens. Henry Lawson was sent to gaol because he couldn't pay his debts. Ended his life begging in the streets of Sydney and did anyone care? Not one. He'd be really amused today if he could see his head on our ten dollar note. Cultural hero — kids study him in schools — ended his life as a joke and nobody cared! It's not going to happen to me. I'm sick of sending scripts off and waiting patiently for the call that never comes and ringing back and ringing back and finally getting someone on the other end of the phone who says, 'Sorry', they haven't had time to read it yet. Being a writer is one of the most humiliating professions on earth and I'm sick to death of it. I want to be a producer, and I want to have money, and I want to have power. I want to sit in my office with people phoning *me*. I want to sit back and tell my secretary that I'm in conference and can't be disturbed and that I'll ring back, then make sure I never do. I want scripts to come to *me*, and *I'll* make the judgements about whether they're good, bad or indifferent. *I'll* be the one with the blue pencil who rips other people's scripts apart, complains about the banality and predictability, groans at the clichéd dialogue, mutters, 'There must be some good writers *somewhere*'. Why *shouldn't* I have money and power? Why *shouldn't* I have a great big house on the waterfront like all the rest of the coked-out mumblers out there masquerading as producers? I want *you* to stop telling people what *I* want out of *my* life, because you are *wrong*! I don't want to make art films or films with a message, I want to produce a product that entertains and I want it to make me awesomely powerful and fabulously rich!

INTERVAL

ACT TWO

KATE *and* COLIN *arrive home.*

KATE: Awesomely powerful and fabulously rich?

COLIN: Yes.

KATE: Colin, I can understand your anxieties, but this isn't the way to handle them. You mustn't compromise your integrity.

COLIN: Of course, you've never compromised your integrity, have you?

KATE: No.

COLIN: No. Your boss told me he was enormously pleased with the ethnic cookbook series you've initiated.

KATE: [*embarrassed*] That's just to give me commercial credibility, so I can do the books I really want to, like *Black Rage.*

COLIN: He told me that the South-East Asian section breaks new ground. What have you got? Fretilin-style snacks for eating on the run? And which one of us insisted on ferreting our daughter through a seventy-year waiting list into the most exclusive girls school in Sydney? Where all her friends live within half a mile of each other in Bellevue Hill, and where she's already planning to graduate at twenty-one, marry at twenty-seven, have two daughters named Francesca and Chloe, divorce her husband at thirty-two and recommence her stockbroking career.

KATE: We couldn't send her to a state school. They're appalling. The system has almost broken down.

COLIN: The state school system is not *nearly* as appalling as guilty socialist mothers who know they shouldn't be stuffing their kids into top private schools would like to believe.

KATE: You went along with it. You came and grovelled in front of the headmistress.

COLIN: I wasn't as low on my belly as you were. [*Imitating* KATE] 'I've been *amazed*, simply *amazed* at how *many* people have told me how *excellent* this school is.' Grovel, grovel. 'I'd be so *happy* if I thought my daughter was being educated in such a *stimulating* intellectual environment.'

KATE: That's really unfair, Colin. It *is* an excellent school academically and if it has got her thinking in terms of career independence —

COLIN: [*interrupting*] Career independence? It's turning her into a predatory neo-feminist socialite. She and her friends know the name of every eligible private school boy in Sydney. They swap descriptions and wealth assessments of ones they've never even met. Australia a classless society? There's selective breeding out there in the Eastern suburbs that would make our pedigree stud farms look like amateurs, and our daughter is in the thick of it. Do you know that she hasn't met one boy who goes to a state school since she came to Sydney? I said to her, 'Do you realise that *I* went to a state school? If I was your age you would never have met me.' She said, 'Good.'

KATE: If you feel so strongly about it, take her out of there.

COLIN: She's settled in. She likes it.

KATE: And you like it too, if the truth be known. State school boy's daughter gets to top private school.

COLIN: I am *riddled* with compromise and ambivalence. At least I admit it.

KATE: My primary purpose in sending her there was to give her a good education!

COLIN: You rage at the fact that thousands in this city are homeless, yet you send your daughter to be educated in an atmosphere that'll teach her not to give a damn!

KATE: [*angrily, defensively*] Take her out of there then.

COLIN: *You* take her out. You're supposed to be the one with the social conscience!

KATE: She'll see through all that phony Bellevue Hill stuff.

COLIN: You want her there because it's a top private school too. You're one of that vast army of fake altruists who condemn the filthy rich and mouth platitudes about the sufferings of the underprivileged, then go along and collect their fat paychecks every week and never do a damn thing about it. Well, I've stopped pretending. I'm going to be a producer and become enormously powerful and *disgustingly* rich!

KATE: If I wasn't so appalled, I'd laugh.

COLIN: Would you? Why?

KATE: You can't even do the shopping without forgetting half of it.

COLIN: What's that got to do with it?

KATE: You forget my birthday, the kids birthdays, and every second appointment you make.

COLIN: Producing involves more than attention to petty detail.

KATE: That's got to be *part* of it, surely?

COLIN: It's picking the right projects. Knowing scripts.

KATE: The kids have got to repeat every question they ask you because you're off in another world. Our credit cards are always bouncing and we're always about to lose either the telephone, electricity or the gas because you never remember to pay. You had to hire a line producer on *Coastwatchers* to get you out of the mess.

COLIN: It was just inexperience.

KATE: That fiasco over the extras —

COLIN: [*interrupting*] I wrote '*Forty* Japanese burst from the clearing.' Mike got it wrong.

KATE: Most producers would have spotted the error before a chartered Jumbo with four hundred extras arrived from Tokyo. Colin, you just haven't got the right temperament to be a producer. You turned grey during *Coastwatchers* and I couldn't sleep at night because you were rotating like a corkscrew, shouting abuse at Mike in your sleep.

COLIN: *He's* the reason we had to get a line producer. Never did a bloody thing.

KATE: And you're going to work with him again?

COLIN: He'd better shape up this time and he knows it.

KATE: You've spoken to him?

COLIN: He knows it. He knows I'm not happy.

KATE: Colin, *I* know when you're not happy. You tap your right foot and clench your right fist, but it's taken eighteen years of marriage to spot the signals. Mike is so insensitive he'd be hard-put to spot the irritation on the face of a charging tiger.

COLIN: He *knows* I'm not happy.

KATE: Colin, I wish you'd look at the situation honestly.

Mike's a downmarket hustler and you're a writer. You might end up begging on the streets of Sydney but it's a chance you're going to have to take. You're absent-minded and vague because your brain's always away somewhere else working on plotlines and dialogue. You wake up at night and tell me stories you've dreamt. You mustn't try and be what you're not.

COLIN: Stick in the same old rut. Let yourself be kicked from pillar to post.

KATE: You can't do something that's not in your nature.

COLIN: I'll decide what my nature is, not you.

KATE: A producer has to be ruthless.

COLIN: I can be ruthless. I'm going to be the most ruthless bastard in this city.

KATE: Colin, you're about as ruthless as a toothless old pussycat.

COLIN: You're wrong. I'm going to be so ruthless you wouldn't believe.

[KATE *exits and* MIKE *enters.* COLIN *sits and listens to* MIKE. *They're at* MIKE*'s place.*]

MIKE: Right. There's these two undercover cops in Darlinghurst. Prostitutes, drugs — all of that sort of stuff going on around them. These aren't your typical cops. These guys are young, spunky, wear the latest fashions and the art direction gives us everything in pastel shades and there's a lot of action and car chases and a rock soundtrack.

COLIN: You're three years too late. That's *Miami Vice.*

MIKE: No, it's different.

COLIN: How's it different?

[*Pause.*]

MIKE: Right. There's this career woman divorced with a young kid. She gets someone in to housekeep and he's a guy and *he's* got a kid —

COLIN: [*interrupting*] Where'd that come from?

MIKE: There's a show a bit similar in the States, but this'll be set in Australia.

COLIN: Mike, we have to do something *original.*

MIKE: There's nothing new under the sun, mate. All we can do is add a new twist.

COLIN: I don't believe that.

MIKE: A series about a D.J.

COLIN: Sitting there playing records?

MIKE: Things are always happening. A gang of Arab terrorists fly in and take over the station.

COLIN: Why would Arab terrorists endure the horrors of a twenty-four hour Qantas flight to take over 2GB?

MIKE: [*ignoring the jibe*] They take the D.J. hostage and start making demands.

COLIN: No more talk back? Get rid of John Laws?

MIKE: [*tensely, under pressure*] Release of Arab prisoners.

COLIN: Why are we holding Arab prisoners?

MIKE: We can plug the holes in the plot later. It's the concept.

COLIN: The concept's lousy. We've got to come up with an idea that's brilliantly original and commercial. We can't afford another lemon like *Coastwatchers*.

[HELEN *enters the room looking tantalisingly sexy.* COLIN *tries to disugise his interest, but finds it hard not to stare at her.*]

HELEN: Working late?

MIKE: Two coffees, love.

HELEN: [*to* COLIN] Black with one sugar?

COLIN: Please.

HELEN: No, it's not. It's black with *no* sugar isn't it?

COLIN: It is actually. I wasn't thinking.

HELEN: Head like a sieve. I can never remember things like that.

COLIN: Neither can I.

HELEN: Names too. I'm hopeless with names.

COLIN: So am I. Introductions are a nightmare.

HELEN: Really? You always look so assured and confident.

COLIN: Me?

HELEN: When you get one of your awards or something on T.V.

COLIN: Shaking like a jelly.

HELEN: There's hope for me.

MIKE: How'd it go today?

HELEN: Disaster.

[*She turns to* COLIN *to explain. During the explanation* COLIN *doesn't take in one word. He watches the expressions on her face, transfixed.*]

I was hired to organise the publicity for Rod Miki — heard
of him?

[COLIN *shakes his head.*]

Neither had anyone else. He's a new-wave comedian from
L.A. who's about as funny as a funeral.

COLIN: You had a problem.

HELEN: Did I ever. By the time I picked him up he'd finished
his first bottle of whiskey; he tried to get my top off, I hit
the car in front and when we got to the first interview he
lay on the floor and screamed at the journo to jump on him.

COLIN: Jump on him?

HELEN: He said she'd only come to put the boot in — why
didn't she do the job properly?

MIKE: Jesus!

HELEN: What was I supposed to do? He was uncontrollable.

MIKE: You should have told him that the journo thought he
was a genius.

HELEN: It's a bit hard to spread disinformation when you're
being raped in peak-hour traffic in George Street.

MIKE: If you didn't wear gear that opened you for public
inspection, you wouldn't have that sort of problem. Two
coffees! Do you think you can do that without getting
yourself raped?

[HELEN *glares, turns and goes.*]

COLIN: [*to the audience*] Why did she put up with it? She
deserved someone sensitive, intelligent — someone who sat
and marvelled as the passions passed like summer storms
across the face of her beauty. She deserved me, but I didn't
know how to make the offer. In the past I'd been so inept
and shy that I always waited for the woman to give the first
sign in case I made a fool of myself, but this time it was
too urgent for that. I didn't want to wreck my marriage,
I just wanted a heady, passionate affair, but if I made an
approach and she refused, she'd be sure to tell Mike, and
if she accepted, knowing my luck, Kate would find out and
be off to her room in Glebe like a flash. I didn't know what
to do, but I knew I had to do something. Every time she
spoke, every time she did *anything* including standing stock
still, I was overpoweringly attracted.

[COLIN *exits.* ELAINE *enters at a cocktail party. Chatter and the clinking of glasses can be heard.* ELAINE *stands by herself with a glass in her hand.* MIKE *approaches her.*]

MIKE: Mike McCord.

ELAINE: [*frostily*] Oh, yes. You're working with Colin.

MIKE: [*nodding*] Getting a few projects together.

ELAINE: Good.

MIKE: You?

ELAINE: Getting a few projects together too.

MIKE: Good.

[*There is an awkward pause.* ELAINE *doesn't want to continue the conversation, but* MIKE *stands there doggedly.*]

MIKE: Ned Wiseman's film's a disaster.

ELAINE: [*interested despite herself*] Really?

MIKE: They put it in the third house at the Hoyts complex and it only did seven thousand.

ELAINE: The first day?

MIKE: The first week.

ELAINE: That's a disaster.

MIKE: Total. Have you seen it?

ELAINE: Bad?

MIKE: A character says, 'I don't know why we're doing this,' and the audience yells, 'Neither do we.'

ELAINE: [*trying to hide her glee*] How sad for Ned. I quite liked *Coastwatchers*.

MIKE: Could've been better.

ELAINE: It lacked momentum.

MIKE: [*nodding*] Right.

ELAINE: Second half was a little better.

MIKE: [*nodding*] A lot of that was mine.

ELAINE: You wrote the second half?

MIKE: We were both still in on it, but Colin ran out of steam.

ELAINE: The second half was quite strong. Emotionally.

MIKE: Had to fight for that. Emotion embarrasses Colin.

ELAINE: Yes, it does, doesn't it?

MIKE: Prefers things clinical and distant. With me it's emotion, emotion, emotion all the way. Colin's a bit cold.

ELAINE: As a person?

MIKE: [*nodding*] Never seems to get stirred up by anything.

ELAINE: No, he doesn't.

MIKE: Shows up in his writing.

ELAINE: I've never thought of it like that, but you could be right. The second half was a lot stronger emotionally.

MIKE: [*shrugging, taking credit*] Well, if you don't know when to put the accelerator down, you shouldn't be driving the car. Whenever I write a scene I ask myself one simple question: 'What's at stake? Who stands to lose, who stands to gain?' Unless something's at stake all you've got is two people chatting.

ELAINE: That makes a lot of sense, Ian.

MIKE: Mike.

ELAINE: Sorry. Mike.

MIKE: Those films you made with Colin. How much of the horsepower and the emotion came from you?

ELAINE: An enormous amount. An enormous amount. You can't skirt around anguish and you can't skirt around pain, and I made him take back those scripts and rewrite and rewrite until we got it.

MIKE: It shows.

ELAINE: Not that he's ever thanked me for it. I'm not denying that he's a very talented writer, but I had to ride shotgun over him to ensure we felt something.

MIKE: It shows.

ELAINE: Not that he ever thanked me for it. Did you ever see *Days of Wine and Whitlam?*

MIKE: [*nodding*] Good movie.

ELAINE: Do you remember how big Stewart Egan was then? International rock star — every producer in the country offering him roles and every one of them being turned down flat. I saw him *seventeen* times before he agreed to do it. *Seventeen* times, and he finally signed. It *made* that film and it *made* Colin. Now, can you believe this? Without a word of warning, Colin turned on me last year and launched an *incredible* tirade about how I'd compromised the film because Egan was a rock star. Can you believe that? Can you believe that?

MIKE: [*shifting uneasily*] Turned on you?

ELAINE: [*gritting her teeth*] I said to myself, 'You ungrateful

swine. You ungrateful bloody *swine*.' And then he had the
gall to tell me Scranton was the wrong choice of director.

MIKE: [*uneasily*] Really.

ELAINE: [*gritting her teeth*] I thought to myself, 'You conceited
young swine. You were damn lucky to get him. Damn lucky
to get him.'

MIKE: Scranton names his own price in Hollywood these
days.

ELAINE: I thought to myself, 'Let's see you have the guts to
land in Los Angeles without a penny and make it to the
top like Scranton.' It took years to talk Colin into coming
as far as Sydney.

MIKE: Perhaps he knows he wouldn't make it over there.

ELAINE: Exactly.

MIKE: If there's one thing Hollywood demands, it's emotion.

ELAINE: [*grudgingly*] He's got talent.

MIKE: Sure.

ELAINE: But severe limitations.

MIKE: Yep.

[ELAINE *looks slightly ashamed of herself for having said so
much.*]

ELAINE: Must go and meet this director. What is he,
Yugoslav?

MIKE: Pole. Don't bother.

ELAINE: You've seen his film?

[MIKE *nods.*]

ELAINE: A little slow?

MIKE: [*nodding*] Starts at a crawl and gallops to a standstill.

[ELAINE *smiles, turns to go away, then turns back*].

ELAINE: Are you and Colin working on your projects full-
time, or do you have some time to spare?

MIKE: Always got time to spare if the project's good.

ELAINE: I've got a *very* good project. I should talk to you about
it.

MIKE: I'll give you a ring.

[ELAINE *exits.*]

[*To the audience*] I'd worked out by this time that
collaborating with Colin was leading nowhere. He didn't
have a gut feel for the commercial and never would. I had

my doubts about Elaine too. Pompous old chook, with more
venom than the reptile house at the zoo, but she still had
a reputation around the traps, and when the word got round
that I was working on one of her projects, the *real* offers
would start coming in.

    [MIKE *exits.* COLIN *speaks to* HELEN *in another corner of the
room. He's consumed with desire and trying desperately to conceal
it.*]

COLIN: I don't normally come to these things.

HELEN: I have to. I'm organising the P.R. for this guy.

COLIN: Must be difficult to crank yourself up into a state of
enthusiasm if you don't really feel it.

HELEN: Can be, but this guy's really nice. Have you met
him?

COLIN: I haven't seen his film yet, so I'm too embarrassed.

HELEN: It's really good. I know I'm being paid to say that,
but it really is.

COLIN: I must see it.

HELEN: [*nodding*] It's about this guy who loves his wife like
crazy — even though she's a bit off, behaviourwise. Manic
depressive or something. She falls in love with a truck driver
and goes off with him and feels really guilty about it, but
it's compulsive and she can't really help herself — you
know?

COLIN: [*nodding*] Right.

HELEN: The husband is *absolutely* devastated. There's this one
scene that would have to be one of the most moving scenes
I've ever seen on film.

    [COLIN *nods.*]

The husband just sits there crying for two minutes and the
camera doesn't move. I sat there bawling my eyes out. Can
you imagine an Australian writer or director having the
guts to do anything as sensitive as that.

COLIN: [*melancholy*] If an Australian writer scripted something
like that it just wouldn't get made. The distributors and
merchant bankers and network execs who run this industry
wouldn't bother to read the script. All they want is money,
lust, power, crime, fashion, intrigue, murder, jewellery and
crocodiles.

HELEN: I know. I feel disloyal saying it, but I hate some of the Australian product I've had to promote.

COLIN: I hate it too, but Mike and I are writing one to exactly the same formula. It's fine for the Poles. They don't have to face commercial pressures.

HELEN: They have to face other kinds. The Ministry of Culture watches this guy like a hawk. He nearly went to prison after his last film because his main character was a corrupt party official.

COLIN: Really?

HELEN: Colin, I'm going to say something to you I shouldn't say.

COLIN: Please do.

HELEN: I don't think your partnership with Mike is good for either of you.

COLIN: Why not?

HELEN: Mike's at home with power, lust, murder and crocodiles and I'm not knocking him for it. We all have to earn a living. People in glass houses. But occasionally, when I've seen a film like that, I wish I lived in a better world where I could say what I felt and mean what I say, and you can write films like that and I think you should.

COLIN: Yes, I should. And you should be doing something better than selling people and products you don't believe in.

HELEN: Yes, I should.

COLIN: I have to say this, and I don't care how corny it sounds. You are one of the most beautiful women I have ever seen.

[HELEN *looks into his eyes.* COLIN *becomes nervous, manic.*]
[*Talking rapidly*] When you first walked into the room, I just stood there dumbstruck. Absolutely dumbstruck. You must have noticed.

HELEN: I did sense there was an extraordinary affinity between us. Right from the start.

COLIN: There was. An *extraordinary* affinity. And all I did was stand there, mouth agape. Instead of trusting the feeling that you were feeling what I was feeling, I began feeling that I might be wrong. Why is it that at the moment we should throw caution to the wind, we're struck deaf mute with panic?

HELEN: Do you want to stay here long?

COLIN: I suppose you have to stick around here until the end?

HELEN: I should, but to hell with it. Let's go and book into a hotel.

COLIN: Hotel? Yes. Hotel. What's a good hotel on this side of the city.

HELEN: We'll find one.

COLIN: Helen, this is crazy. This is really crazy.

HELEN: Crazy, but right.

COLIN: Did I bring the car? Yes, of course I did. Hotels. Where are we? North Sydney. Hotel. Jesus, my mind is a total blank. God, I *didn't* bring the car. We'll get a cab. There is quite a nice hotel somewhere over in Manly. God, no, that's miles away. Artarmon! On the highway just down the road. Do you know the one I mean?

HELEN: No.

COLIN: No. It's actually pretty appalling. No, there's no way we're going to go there.

HELEN: There must be dozens of places within a few miles of here. Let's just get a cab and cruise.

COLIN: [*suddenly pulling a set of car keys out of his pocket*] Jesus, I *did* bring the car. *I am going crazy.* Can you believe that? I *did* bring the car.

HELEN: Great. Let's go then.

COLIN: What about Mike?

HELEN: You go down first. I'll think of an excuse then follow. [COLIN *hesitates.*]

HELEN: Do you want to go, or don't you?

COLIN: [*to the audience*] I couldn't do it. In the seventies you could wreck marriages and traumatise kids and call it personal growth. In the eighties we realised that personal growth was a polite term for self indulgence.

HELEN: [*to the audience*] What a bummer. Still, you can't win 'em all.

COLIN: [*to the audience, berating himself*] Gutless, pathetic, pathologically timid! But it probably was just as well.

[*They stare at each other in the moonlight, nod, and finally part. They exit. Some time later* COLIN *walks into his living room.* KATE *sits there with an inscrutable look on her face.* COLIN *looks agitated and annoyed. As always, when worked up about something,* COLIN *patrols up and down gesticulating as he speaks.*]

KATE: What's wrong?

COLIN: Kate, what am I doing with my life. I've just been to a film commission cocktail party and met a Polish director who works under daily threat and yet he makes masterpieces! I have every freedom in the world and I'm writing shit!

KATE: Not quite *every* freedom. The money men won't look at anything that's not sex, sadism or sensation.

COLIN: [*at a peak of gesticulation*] That's the *excuse* I use to justify what I'm doing, but honestly, isn't it just that? An excuse? A justification? Couldn't I fight harder? Couldn't I batter at the walls? Couldn't I keep going back, bloody and wounded until I found *someone* in this merciless money maze who asked what *sort* of film he was putting his money into, rather than the rate of return he thinks he'll get? There must be rich men with the souls of artists out there and it's my responsibility to find them. Why don't I? Why don't I try?

KATE: Apparently because you want money and power.

COLIN: I don't want money and power!

KATE: You did yesterday.

COLIN: I don't any longer.

KATE: Good. Want to know my news?

COLIN: What?

KATE: *Black Rage*'s been selected as a finalist in the Booker prize.

COLIN: The Booker?

KATE: [*nodding*] Everyone in the office went beserk, and guess who was the first to congratulate me? Ian. The man who opposed it all the way.

COLIN: [*dully*] That's great.

KATE: I'm being flown over there.

COLIN: To London?

KATE: [*nodding*] We've got to be represented in case we win.

COLIN: What about the author?

KATE: She'll be there too. They're flying us first class.

COLIN: First class? I've never flown anywhere first class in my life.

KATE: The Booker is big time, my dear. Big time. Just in being *nominated* will double our sales and there'll be *huge* sales in the states if we win. *Huge* sales. When Tom Keneally won the Booker, Stephen Spielberg bought the film rights.

COLIN: [*moral outrage sparked*] Wait a minute? Hang on there! Wasn't *Black Rage* going to be the book that was only going to sell a thousand or two but seep slowly into our consciousness? Stephen Spielberg? What kind of film will Stephen Spielberg make? Aliens descending in spaceships to take our downtrodden Aboriginals off to a loving, more equitable planet? Where are your ideals, woman? What's happened to your ideals?

KATE: [*defensively*] Nothing!

　　　[COLIN *picks up a brochure* KATE *has brought in with her. He reads it.*]

COLIN: Thai Airways? You're going to be met at the doorway by an 'elegant and courteous stewardess attired in traditional Thai dress, and offered your choice of French Champagne or orange juice and delicious satay beef cubes and crab claws to nibble on.' How wonderful for you.

KATE: For once in my life I'm going to have a little bit of luxury and enjoy it.

COLIN: You're living in a city in which thousands are homeless!

KATE: I can't do anything about it in the short term, can I?

COLIN: Not when you're thirty thousand feet up nibbling crab's claws, no.

KATE: I voted for the government that should be doing something about it. It's not my fault that they aren't.

COLIN: You found out that Sue Michaelis had flown first class, and asked her how she could ever justify the fact that the extra ten cubic feet of body space she had bought herself for twenty-four hours, would have kept eight families in Bangladesh alive for a year.

KATE: I was a little fanatical in those days.

COLIN: That was just last year.

KATE: Colin, whether I travel first class or not, the familes in Bangladesh aren't going to get any extra money.

COLIN: They would if you cashed in your first class ticket, went tourist, and sent Freedom from Hunger the difference.

KATE: Colin, I'm feeling guilty enough already. Don't make me feel any worse. The minute I have any success in my career you get nasty.

COLIN: I'm not getting nasty. I'm just pointing out that it only takes one first class ticket and your ferocious moral standards take a nosedive.

KATE: Colin, this book has been one of my great triumphs. Can't you be a little bit generous?

COLIN: Triumph? A mouldy little book in an overrated competition? I'm just about to become the first foreign producer ever to sell a series to prime time television in the United States.

KATE: What kind of an achievement is that? Prime time television in America is to art what McDonalds is to cooking.

COLIN: Which would you rather have a percentage of? Maxim's or McDonalds?

KATE: Colin, I think you're coming apart at the seams. You came in here ranting with Polish-fired zeal, determined to make films of quality, and now you're bursting with pride because you're about to sell schlock to N.B.C. What's going on in your head?

COLIN: [*gesticulating wildly*] I wish I knew! One minute I want to make a film that's so beautiful and truthful and angry and funny that people in this country who still *care* about justice and truth and compassion will leave the cinema weeping, and the next minute my head is full of images of mansions on the waterfront. I know what I *should* do! Reject the false gods — but it's not that easy! We live in a culture that *worships* wealth and *worships* power and gives artistic success no recognition or honour of any kind!

KATE: Colin, you're being a *little* bit overdramatic.

COLIN: [*overdramatically*] Am I? Am I? What do you have at the end of your life to show for your artistic success? An

old age pension, a one bar radiator — if you can afford
the fuel bills — and a few yellowing crits in a dusty
scrapbook. It's too demeaning, Kate. It's too bloody
demeaning! If I've got to choose between money and
oblivion, I'll take the money!

[KATE *exits.* COLIN *sits at* MIKE*'s place. He dictates, or
attempts to dictate, the script to* MIKE *as of old, but there's a
subtle change.* MIKE *is offering resistance.*]

Let's have a close-up of him kick-starting the bike.

MIKE: Kick-start shots went out with *Easy Rider.*

[MIKE *taps out a few lines rapidly.*]

COLIN: [*tersely*] What was that you wrote?

MIKE: Just a thought I had.

COLIN: What?

MIKE: Catch up with it later.

COLIN: [*quietly fuming*] If kick shots went out with Easy Rider,
what do you suggest?

MIKE: Zoom in on the helmet going on with a snap and pan
down across his body to the exhaust pipe belching fumes.

COLIN: [*considering this reluctantly*] All right. Write it.

MIKE: I've written it.

COLIN: [*trying to regain control*] Right, now before Grant rides
off he should turn and say —

MIKE: [*interrupting*] Don't need any dialogue. The intention's
clear.

COLIN: [*clenched teeth*] I'd like him to make the point —

MIKE: [*interrupting*] You wouldn't hear what he was saying in
any case over the exhaust and the rock track.

COLIN: What are we making here? A cartoon? We're twenty
minutes into the episode and only twelve words have been
spoken.

MIKE: This is an eighties series in a visual medium, mate. If
you can't tell your story in images, don't tell it at all.

COLIN: Mike, we share ninety-nine percent of our D.N.A.
with the chimpanzee. The bonus of that extra one percent
is language. An astonishing facility for language. There
are sixteen distinct meanings for the word 'beat', but we
can instantly recognise which of the sixteen is intended by
context. When the most advanced language computer tried

to translate, 'The spirit is willing but the flesh is weak' into
Russian, it came out 'The vodka's strong, but the veal is
pallid'.

MIKE: What point are you trying to make?

COLIN: How can we ever know our characters if they're never
allowed to speak? We're writing a series about chimpanzees!
Before you can be interested in a character, you've got to
know how they speak and think, how they justify what
they're doing, to themselves and to each other, how they
cope with the big questions: life, death and meaning; how
they view the tragic irony of being transient specks of living
matter in an infinite and incomprehensible universe!

MIKE: O.K. What do you want him to say?

   [COLIN *thinks.*]

COLIN: 'We'd better check this one out, Zac.'

   [MIKE *hesitates, then taps it out.* COLIN *frowns and stares at*
   MIKE. *He doesn't understand the new assertiveness.* MALCOLM,
   the merchant banker, enters some weeks later. COLIN *and* MIKE
   stand in front of him. MALCOLM *has a thick script in his hand.*]

MALCOLM: [*indicating the script*] You really think this is going
to sell to a U.S. network?

COLIN: Yes.

MALCOLM: You've sent the script across?

COLIN: Yes.

MALCOLM: You've had some response?

COLIN: Nothing definite, but a high level of interest.

MALCOLM: From who?

COLIN: The reader at N.B.C. said she found the concept
intriguing.

MALCOLM: The concept is five years too late. It's *Miami Vice*
down under.

COLIN: On the surface it's a little similar —

MALCOLM: [*interrupting*] Colin, this is the seventh *Miami Vice*
I've been given in the last sixth months.

COLIN: There are a lot of novel twists. One of the cops, Zac,
is a Ph.D.

MALCOLM: In Astrophysics? A cop in Darlinghurst? And the
other's an ex-world surfing champion and cordon bleue
cook? Colin, this is *shit*.

COLIN: So is *Miami Vice.*

MALCOLM: That's classy shit. This is *absolute* shit.

COLIN: I can't see the difference.

MALCOLM: Which is exactly why the chances of you getting a network sale are about the same as the monkey accidently typing *Hamlet.* The writers of *Miami Vice* don't sit down and say to themselves, 'I am going to write shit.' They write at the highest level they're capable of and when they finish they think they've written a masterpiece. When someone who can write at a higher level tries to imitate them it's a disaster.

COLIN: [*taking the script*] I hope you're big enough to admit that you were wrong.

MALCOLM: I'll be delighted to admit I was wrong. You get a pre-sale from the Americans, we'll finance.

> [COLIN *glowers and moves towards the door.* MIKE *turns to follow.*]

[*to* MIKE] That project you're working on with Elaine Ross sounds like something we'd be interested in, Mike.

MIKE: [*embarrassed*] Oh. Right.

MALCOLM: Send me a script when it's done.

> [MALCOLM *exits.* COLIN *and* MIKE *stand outside the office.*]

COLIN: What's the script you're doing for Elaine?

MIKE: [*embarrassed*] It's about a guy whose kids die in a fun park accident. Said she offered it to you and you turned it down.

COLIN: I couldn't see a film in it. Seemed like a worn-out theme to me.

MIKE: I think it's strong. I think it's a winner.

COLIN: [*waving the script*] We'll get *this* one up. He's not the only merchant banker in town.

MIKE: That's the game we're in. When it's hot, run with it, when it's cold, bail out.

COLIN: We've spent months on it. We're not giving up yet.

MIKE: It's dead, mate.

> [MIKE *exits,* KATE *enters.* COLIN *paces up and down.* KATE *watches him.*]

COLIN: I can't believe it. He's never written anything and Elaine's got him working on a script she really cares about.

KATE: It's exactly what I told you would happen.

COLIN: He's never written a thing in his life!

KATE: He's the co-writer of *Coastwatchers*.

COLIN: Everyone knows he couldn't have written any of that.

KATE: Do they? How?

COLIN: They know *my* record. They know *his*.

KATE: What do you think Mike's been doing out there since *Coastwatchers*, Colin? Going around the cocktail circuit admitting that he didn't write a word?

COLIN: I'm the only writer in the country who could do that script of Elaine's. It's got to have characters that are *individual* and who *live*. Elaine must be off her head.

KATE: You can't expect her to wait around forever when you turn her down flat.

COLIN: I would have done it eventually.

KATE: You're *impossibly* arrogant sometimes, Colin. She's expected to wait round for ever on the off-chance?

COLIN: If I can't get this series into production I'll have no money coming in all next year.

KATE: Not to worry.

COLIN: Not to worry? Do you know how much Penny's school fees are now?

[KATE *nods*. COLIN *examines her narrowly*.]

COLIN: Have you been drinking?

KATE: I've had a few glasses of champagne. I've just got a forty percent rise.

COLIN: Forty percent?

KATE: It won't be that much after tax.

COLIN: Forty percent?

KATE: I've been promoted.

COLIN: To what? You're only two rungs under God now.

KATE: Ian's become national manager. I've got his job.

COLIN: [*choking on the words*] Congratulations. That's wonderful.

KATE: I get his old office on the seventeenth floor. You see the whole harbour.

COLIN: Really.

KATE: You must come up and have a look. On a sunny day when the eighteen footers are out, the combination of

striped spinnaker, sparkling blue water and sky is *absolutely*
overwhelming. I don't know how I'm ever going to get any
work done.

COLIN: That's wonderful.

KATE: You were right about Sydney. It's the most exciting
city in the *world*. I couldn't live anywhere else. [*To the
audience*] I've got to be honest. I loved that moment. Deep
at the heart of every marriage between professionals there's
a struggle for supremacy, and if one partner gets too far
ahead for too long, the marriage goes sour. Colin had had
his years of being lionised. It was my turn.

COLIN: [*dully*] Will you still be going to London?

KATE: Oh, yes. And the promotion means my living expenses
go up by seventy dollars a day. I'll be able to have a ball.

COLIN: [*dully*] Great.

KATE: [*to the audience*] Marriages can be awful. Right when
your partner's at his lowest ebb, you sink in the boot. I'm
not proud in retrospect, but at the time I *loved* it.

[KATE *and* COLIN *exit.* MIKE *and* HELEN *enter.* MIKE *talks
on the telephone.* HELEN *watches him.*]

MIKE: [*into the phone*] Sounds great. Why don't I come around
and we'll talk about it?

[*Pause.*]

Yep. That's fine. See you then.

[*He hangs up and notes down the time and place in his diary.*]

[*Exultantly*] Terry Severino wants me to write a movie for
him.

HELEN: Mike, you can't take on any more work. You're
doing five already.

MIKE: When you're hot, you run with it. Next week you
might be colder than Melbourne in May.

HELEN: How are you going to finish any of them?

MIKE: I'll manage.

HELEN: You'll kill yourself.

MIKE: Honey, it's make or break time. They've thrown me
the ball and I've got to run with it.

HELEN: Look at your hand shaking.

MIKE: [*taking tablets*] You want to live in this dump all your
life?

HELEN: Don't take any more of those tablets, Mike. You're stomach'll dissolve.

MIKE: Add up the numbers in the contracts I've signed in the last two months and it comes to more than I've earned in the last ten years.

HELEN: Look, I know I give you a hard time about this house, but —

MIKE: [*interrupting*] Honey, you are '*un poule superieux*'.

HELEN: A what?

MIKE: A top chook. You could've had any guy in this city, and don't think I don't know it. I am going to put you in a mansion on the waterfront with a boat moored outside, because anything less is an insult.

HELEN: Mike —

MIKE: [*interrupting*] Honey, there are women out there with a tenth of what you've got who've treated me like shit. How do you say, 'Thank you' to someone who's given you more than you ever hoped for and much more than you deserve? This is the only way I know how.

HELEN: Mike, I'm really moved, and I am, believe me, but I'd much rather be living here with you, than sitting in a waterfront while you're in intensive care.

MIKE: Honey, for the first time in my life I've found a game I might win. Suddenly, there's a doorway, and I've got a foot in, and I can see myself through and on the other side and nobody's putting me down any more, and do you know what that's like to me? That's like being in heaven. Bliss.

   [HELEN *exits.*]

[*To the audience*] Problem is, when you take on half a dozen big jobs at once, you do eventually have to deliver. I started living on a diet of milk and indigestion tablets and as the telephone calls started coming in my brain log-jammed with fear and dread. No shortage of ideas. Brilliant ideas. But between the idea and the typewriter something happened. There was some freak circuit in my brain that, right at the last moment, in the instant before the idea hit the paper, turned gold into shit. I was in a waking nightmare. I was a grand opera singer who hears the nightingale inside her

head, opens her mouth, and out comes the croak of a frog.
The phone kept ringing and I extended the dates again,
and again. My brain was on the point of exploding. My
stomach already had. I looked down, teetering on the brink
of the success I'd always dreamed of and saw the crocodiles
below. There *had* to be a way out. *Had* to.

[MALCOLM *enters.*]

MALCOLM: I raise finance, Mike. I don't want to get involved
in production.

MIKE: Malcolm, listen. Let's have a long hard look at this
industry of ours. Over four hundred films in the last ten
years and only *one* has done big business where it counts:
in the U.S.

MALCOLM: It's a hard market to crack.

MIKE: It shouldn't be, Malcolm. We've been failing because
we've been going about it in a half-arsed way. We bring
over a few faded American stars and plonk them in a cliché-
ridden Australian wank, and think we've made something
international. We'll *never* make true international product
that way. We have to go the whole hog. A big production
house with ten or twelve projects going at once and *everything*
international. International scripts, international stars,
international directors. Malcolm, there's no reason why
Australia couldn't become one of the world's great
production houses. Climates better than California,
technicians are much cheaper. Got good local actors for
the supporting roles.

MALCOLM: The Americans can't understand their accents.

MIKE: Bring out tutors. Voice coaches. It can be done,
Malcolm. I swear to you, it can be done. The Canadians
make better American movies than the Americans, and the
reason they succeed is that they don't feel they have to make
pissant little movies about the Canadian way of life. We'll
have all the Advance Aussie patriots having hernia's
because we put American numberplates on Aussie cars,
but stuff 'em, Malcolm. Stuff 'em. If we'd just be honest
with ourselves for a change, we'd admit that our accent
is bloody awful for the simple reason that we never open
our bloody mouths. It was good enough in the old days

when Grandad was out in the bush and had to keep the flies out, but it's *death* to the international saleability of our product.

MALCOLM: What's the precise deal you're suggesting, Mike?

MIKE: You pay expenses to get me to L.A. so I can line up the talent and do the deals. Every project I get up we split the profits fifty-fifty. If I don't get anything up, all you've lost is a few plane fares.

MALCOLM: You're convinced it could work?

MIKE: The world's a global village, Malcolm. A merchant banker in New York has got far more in common with you than a sheep farmer from Walgett, right?

MALCOLM: [*nodding*] It's high time we stopped being so bloody parochial.

MIKE: [*nodding*] Stuff the gumnut cliqué. Let's start making hard-headed, rational business decisions for a change. The North American market is three hundred million, ours is fifteen. Where does the future lie?

[MIKE *and* MALCOLM *exit.* COLIN *and* KATE *enter.* COLIN *reads a newspaper. He puts it down like a man who's been hit in the solar plexus.*]

COLIN: [*in a strangled voice*] Kate, this is like a nightmare.

KATE: What?

COLIN: Malcolm Bennett and Mike McCord have just floated a joint production company with a hundred million dollars worth of projects slated for the coming year.

KATE: Is there some other Mike McCord?

COLIN: God forbid.

KATE: Why would Bennett go into partnership with —

COLIN: [*interrupting*] Why did I go into partnership with him? He's Mephistopheles doing the rounds of the industry.

KATE: [*reading the paper*] They will make films that will 'compete on the international market without sacrificing their essential ''Australianness''.'

COLIN: I feel devastated.

KATE: I don't wonder.

COLIN: I feel as if, suddenly, I don't know how the world works any more. There are producers all over the city screaming for scripts he hasn't finished, and the reason he

didn't finish them, I suspect, is that if he ever did, he'd
be revealed as a total charlatan. He's risen to the top on
the basis of *Coastwatchers*, in which he hardly wrote a line,
and six scripts that no one has ever seen! In the sort of world
I can comprehend, a man like that wouldn't be up there
deciding our futures.

KATE: He has to be found out eventually.

COLIN: This is the first time in my life I've actually felt I could
kill.

KATE: He has to be found out.

COLIN: I don't think he will. Anyone who can rise so far on
the basis of so little has to be some kind of . . . genius.

> [KATE *exits*. ELAINE *enters at a cocktail party. A background
> of chatter.* ELAINE *stands by herself.* COLIN *walks in and
> practically bumps into her. He looks confused and searches for
> something to say.*]

COLIN: Ah. Elaine. How are things?

ELAINE: [*cuttingly*] Things are fine. I've just taken a third
mortgage out on my house, my bank manager's given me
thirty days to reduce my overdraft by twenty thousand . . .
life is very full and very exciting.

COLIN: [*embarrassed*] Ah. [*Struggling*] Script progressing?

ELAINE: [*with a deadly edge*] Script progressing? Script? You
would possibly be referring to the Sanzari script?

COLIN: Yes.

ELAINE: No.

COLIN: Did Mike finish it?

ELAINE: [*coldly*] Thank you for warning me against him,
Colin.

COLIN: It's not my place —

ELAINE: If you see an old friend about to cast twenty thousand
dollars to the wind, don't you have a slight obligation to
speak a few words of caution? Do you think I enjoy taking
out mortgages?

COLIN: The script was bad?

ELAINE: Script? I got fourteen pages and had to go around
to his flat and *demand* it!

COLIN: Elaine, I couldn't warn you. I've never seen a word
that he's written!

ELAINE: I've seen several, and they're etched on my brain. 'O.K. Rogan, this time the game is up.' 'I've got news for you, Mason: the game has barely begun.' 'I thought you might say that, Rogan, but there's something I think you ought to know: I shuffled the deck. I hold the trumps.'

COLIN: I'm relieved.

ELAINE: I imagine that anyone who didn't have to pay five hundred dollars for that little exchange, would be.

COLIN: I started having nightmares that the man actually had talent. I couldn't find any other explanation for his meteoric rise to the top.

ELAINE: He won't last. [*Reassessing*] He probably will.

COLIN: I'd like to write the Sanzari story, if you're still interested.

ELAINE: I sold the rights.

COLIN: To who?

ELAINE: To Mike McCord.

COLIN: Elaine, you're joking.

ELAINE: I wish I was.

COLIN: You can't be serious. Have you heard about some of the projects they're doing? A fifteen million dollar drama about Lesbian Nuns set in Cincinatti.

ELAINE: Starring Brooke Shields.

COLIN: Why did you sell Sanzari to McCord?

ELAINE: It was the only way I could get my twenty thousand back.

COLIN: Why did I ever come to this city? The water in the harbour's not blue, it's cold and hard and green!

ELAINE: Emerald. The Emerald city of Oz. Everyone comes here along their yellow brick roads looking for the answers to their problems and all they find are the demons within themselves. This city lets 'em out and lets 'em rip.

COLIN: You can't let it off that easily. This city is evil! Glitter, money, fashion, fads, corruption, compromise —

ELAINE: [*interrupting*] Intelligence, professionalism, hard work, standards, flexibility, dedication. It's got the best and the worst, and if you choose the worst, you've only got yourself to blame.

COLIN: [*gesticulating*] There's no forgiveness here. No

compassion! If there isn't a dollar in it, it just doesn't happen.

ELAINE: My daughter teaches handicapped kids on a wage marginally higher than the dole. I keep telling her she's exploited and overworked, but she doesn't want to do anything else. She was born and raised here.

COLIN: Elaine, it's a city that walks over its fallen heroes and picks their pockets on the way!

ELAINE: [*running out of patience*] Go back to Melbourne then, you whinger! Your inner demons won't get you into trouble down there. They couldn't think of anything to suggest! [*Shaking her head*] Brisbane boys are rough as guts, Adelaide's a shade on the prissy side. Perth persons are a worry, but you Melbournians — you're so stuffed full of moral rectitude, the only time you open your mouths is to lecture.

[ELAINE *turns to go away, then turns back.*]

If you're going to stay here, for God's sake go away and write me a screenplay or we'll both be on the dole!

[ELAINE *goes.*]

COLIN: [*to the audience*] Go and write me a screenplay. About what? Critical patience for my observations of middle-class life was running thin. Corruption was passé. The boom area was the underprivileged, the unemployed and exploited minorities. Did I have the depth to identify with their anguish and pain? Did I have the soul? Did I have any alternative?

[KATE *storms in, slamming things around and looking furious. She sees a newspaper* COLIN *has been reading and hurls it in a waste paper basket.*]

COLIN: Something upsetting you?

KATE: Bloody journalists! Have you read it?

COLIN: Certainly have.

KATE: [*staring at him*] Do you agree with her?

COLIN: I think she's got a case.

KATE: She's being totally hysterical!

COLIN: If she doesn't want to sell the film rights, why should she?

KATE: A film will triple the sales of the book.

COLIN: Did you describe the film as being Australia's *The Color Purple?*

KATE: No! I said that *The Color Purple* had shown that films about the mistreatment of minorities could make powerful movies and attract large audiences! She's the one who'll be getting most of the money. We only take twenty percent.

COLIN: She said she had written the book to help her people, not to gain personal fortune or fame.

KATE: She'll just have to cry all the way to the bank.

COLIN: You're going to go ahead and sell the film rights?

KATE: We've sold them.

COLIN: Without her consent?

KATE: Her contract gives us the right to act as her agents. Colin, she's just being hysterical.

COLIN: She says she's scared the film will sensationalise and cheapen what she's written.

KATE: It's sure to be less subtle than the book. Films always are, but it will triple the sales of her novel!

COLIN: Wouldn't it have been smarter to wait and see if she won the Booker? If you're determined to make money with film rights, they'll be worth much more if she wins.

KATE: She's not going to win the Booker. Ian felt it was best to take the offer we had.

COLIN: Who did you sell the rights to?

KATE: [*full of guilt*] I'm sure the film will be hideous, but it will triple the sales of the book, and the book is what is going to have the lasting impact.

COLIN: You didn't sell it to —

KATE: They offered twice as much as anyone else.

[*She sees the look on* COLIN's *face and gets even more defensive.*]
You can't live in a dream world! You've got to take profits into account.

COLIN: Kate, can you imagine what someone with the sensitivity of a Mike McCord will do with *Black Rage*?

KATE: They've got international connections. If the film works in the States, the book will sell in hundreds of thousands.

[*She sees* COLIN's *look.*]
Colin, when you're in a top-level executive position the pressures are enormous. Ian and I have a board of directors to answer to. How am I supposed to explain to them that

we turned down a prime international marketing
opportunity because I don't like Mike McCord?

COLIN: I presume you won't be going to London now?

KATE: [*puzzled, defensive*] Why?

COLIN: Now that you know you're not going to win the
Booker.

KATE: We're not absolutely certain.

COLIN: And now that your author is refusing to go.

KATE: That's her decision.

COLIN: Your boss's secretary phoned.

KATE: What about?

COLIN: She said the Dorchester was confirmed for both of
you.

KATE: [*embarrassed*] Ian's decided to come now that Kath has
pulled out.

COLIN: [*tersely*] Great.

KATE: [*defensively*] Surely you haven't got any worries on that
score.

COLIN: [*tersely*] Why shouldn't I have?

KATE: You've seen him.

COLIN: Yes. He looks like the young Richard Burton.

KATE: He looks like a garden gnome. Colin, grow up. Ours
is a strictly business relationship.
[*to the audience*] He did look more like the young Richard
Burton than a garden gnome, and there had been certain
indications of interest. I had no intention of taking them
up. [*To* COLIN.] Colin, I feel just as badly as you do about
a philistine like Mike getting the film rights, but
unfortunately that's how the commercial world works.

COLIN: I suppose there is a certain justice. Without Mike the
book would never have been published.
[KATE *exits.*]
[*To the audience*] At least I was able to play that one last trump
card on that desolate afternoon. When Kate had left for
London I got a phone call from the person I least expected.
[MIKE *enters and* COLIN *sits in front of him.*]

MIKE: Busy?

COLIN: Not particularly.

MIKE: Done a script for Elaine, I hear.

COLIN: [*nodding*] First draft.

MIKE: What's it about?

COLIN: The victims of corporate greed.

MIKE: Got the money?

COLIN: No.

MIKE: Subject like that might be difficult to raise money on.

COLIN: It will. It's set in Australia, it's saying something important and has characters who spend part of their time outside cars and who occasionally talk.

MIKE: Got something you might be interested in.

COLIN: Really.

MIKE: The Yanks have really gone for *Black Rage*.

COLIN: I'm surprised.

MIKE: Colin, I've got to be honest with you. We've already had a writer working on it, but the script's got a fair way to go.

COLIN: You'd like me to do the changes?

MIKE: There's eighty grand in it for you if you see it through to final draft. It's going to be a big film, Colin. First writer was a hot shot young American and he couldn't come up with the goods. If you can bring it off, it'll make your reputation over there.

COLIN: Why are the Americans interested in the plight of our aboriginals?

MIKE: It's been relocated.

COLIN: Relocated?

MIKE: It's been reset in Tennessee. The characters are black Americans. Richard Pryor is very interested in playing the lead.

COLIN: Mike, do you have the faintest idea why I might not want to take this job?

MIKE: The story is universal. Poverty-stricken black girl grows up to be a human rights lawyer. Could happen anywhere.

COLIN: Mike, there are vast differences between our aborigines and the American blacks.

MIKE: People are people wherever they live, Colin. This is the era of the global village.

COLIN: Not quite. Hundreds of years of separate histories and environments aren't swept away because *Sesame Street* teaches our kids to say, 'Have a nice day.'

MIKE: Colin, nationalism is one of the most destructive of all human forces. Caused countless wars. Billions of deaths.

COLIN: Where are you resetting the Sanzari story? Wyoming?

MIKE: Nebraska, and there might be some work for you on that one too.

COLIN: You're a harlot, mate. You've sold your soul to the highest bidder, and you can stick your eighty grand up your arse!

MIKE: [*puzzled, hurt*] We can't go backwards, mate. I'm flogging myself to within a scalpel's width of major surgery to keep our industry afloat. Trying to generate a hundred million dollar's worth of film making — a fair proportion of which will stay in Australian pockets. How does that make me a harlot? I don't understand your point.

COLIN: [*to the audience*] I wasn't sure I did either. I've always hated flag-waving chauvinism. What's so special about being Australian? What's to rejoice in that I'm a member of this polyglot lot of pale-skinned usurpers who treated their predecessors abominably and resent giving them back some tracts of arid desert and one big rock? Why bother whether we have our own stories or not? My only answer to that is that we have a *right* to them. We are human beings with our own feelings, strengths and weaknesses and we need to know what we are like, and we need to know that we are important enough to have fictions written about us or we will always feel that real life happens somewhere else and is spoken in accents other than our own. But then again, that might be a rationalisation. If there are no Australian stories told I'd be out of a job. If my version of *Miami Vice* had sold to a U.S. network, would I be so virtuous today? Who was I to be judgemental? I thought seriously about relocating *Black Rage* to Tennessee and it started to make a certain amount of sense. Eighty thousand dollars worth of sense. But by the faintest whisker some residual integrity, some deep rooted sense of patriotism, or just the ignominy of having to work for Mike, prevented me doing it.

MIKE: [*to the audience*] The bastard walked out of here and made me feel like a grubby little louse. I sat at my desk and stared into darkness for hours. I finally got up from behind my desk and shouted 'All right! I'm a harlot! Some of us don't have any choice!'

[HELEN *enters.*]

HELEN: I don't think I'll ever get tired of this view. Come and have a look. The eighteen footers have got their spinnakers out.

MIKE: Colin turned down eighty grand today.

HELEN: Colin?

MIKE: I've been hearing stories that he's really down on his luck. Nothing's been happening for him. I get on the phone to L.A. and convince them he's a top writer, which is bloody hard given his current track record. I call him in, offer him the job and he calls me a harlot.

HELEN: Why?

MIKE: Because the story's being relocated to Tennessee.

HELEN: A story's a story wherever it's set.

MIKE: Exactly.

HELEN: I can understand why he might be a bit ...

MIKE: What?

HELEN: Reluctant to work for you.

MIKE: I can't.

HELEN: Now your roles are reversed. It would be a bit hard.

MIKE: So he throws away eighty grand just to spite me? It's insane.

HELEN: Any luck with *Lesbian Nuns?*

MIKE: Got it through last week.

HELEN: You didn't tell me. Did you have to change the script much?

MIKE: A bit. Only one of the nuns is allowed to be lesbian, and it's got to be a tendency. Not consummated.

HELEN: Mike, that's crazy. Isn't the whole point of the story that there are a *lot* of lesbian nuns and they're suffering a hell of a lot of guilt?

MIKE: Honey, you sit at my desk day after day and try and get any film through the American system and you'll realise that what I've done is a bloody miracle.

HELEN: Can't they show the *truth* of anything just for once?

MIKE: Jesus, honey. We get enough truth in our lives. We don't want it up there again on our screens.

HELEN: I know the commercial logic, but occasionally I'd like to see the truth!

MIKE: The only truth that matters in this situation is that they have the money and if they ask me to change nuns into astronauts and lesbian into doughnuts, I will make them a movie about astronauts eating doughnuts. They ask. I give. It's called commerce; it's grubby, and it's how I paid for this view. If you don't like it, we'll go back to Dri-Tot Manor.

HELEN: I just can't believe people wouldn't be interested in a movie about the *real* situation.

MIKE: They probably would, but the men who have the money don't *believe* they would. And that, I'm afraid, is an end to it.

> [MIKE *and* HELEN *exit.* COLIN *enters and sits reading. The doorbell rings.* COLIN *frowns and goes to get it. It's* KATE *with a suitcase.* COLIN *embraces her with passion.*]

KATE: Kids in bed?

COLIN: [*nodding*] Even Penny. Sorry you didn't win.

KATE: I knew we wouldn't. Still.

> [*She shrugs.*]

That was a warm welcome. I'm surprised.

COLIN: So am I. I was planning to be cold and distant.

KATE: Bad time while I was gone?

COLIN: Awful. Shopping without lists is a major trauma, and our daughter's been a monster.

KATE: You said on the phone she had a new boyfriend.

COLIN: Yes.

KATE: He goes to an ordinary high school?

COLIN: Yes.

KATE: That should make you pleased.

COLIN: He was kicked out of his private school for selling dope in the toilets.

KATE: She told you this?

COLIN: No, I listen to the phone calls on the extension. How was the Dorchester?

KATE: Overrated.

COLIN: And the garden gnome?

KATE: [*embarrassed*] Oh, I, er, didn't see much of him. He found himself a native.

COLIN: Black lady?

KATE: English rose. How's work?

COLIN: On to the second draft of the screenplay. No money in sight.

KATE: Tell me something cheerful.

COLIN: I'm very glad to see you home.

KATE: [*to the audience*] And I was very glad to be home. Ian didn't find an English rose. He found me, but what Colin doesn't know won't hurt him. I'd been promoted, I'd been unfaithful, and the marriage was back on an even keel.

COLIN: I did some thinking about the future while you were away. Did you?

KATE: [*guiltily*] Ah. No. It was all a bit frantic.

COLIN: I thought we should go back to Melbourne.

KATE: Melbourne? But Colin —

COLIN: [*interrupting*] But then I changed my mind. Do you know what made me change my mind?

KATE: What?

COLIN: I was waiting for a taxi in the city and there were two derelicts asleep on benches. A City Mission van drove up and a young guy went across and talked to them without any hint of judgement, and took them somewhere safe and warm.

KATE: How does that relate to Melbourne?

COLIN: That young guy doesn't dream of waterfront mansions. He gets a couple of hundred dollars a week, a handful of people know that he's a good human being, and as far as he's concerned, that's enough.

KATE: What are you telling me, Colin? You're going to work for the City Mission.

COLIN: No. I'm not as good a human being as he is, and after the film deal you did on *Black Rage*, neither are you. The incident reminded me of something Elaine said. Don't blame the city. The demons are in *us*.

KATE: So we're going to stay in Sydney?

COLIN: Yes.

KATE: [*drily*] Good. Now that we've settled our future, and you've established that we're both evil, do you think we could go to bed?

> [KATE *exits.* COLIN *stands by himself. Cocktail chatter is heard in the background.* MIKE *enters and walks up to him.*]

MIKE: Finally got that film of yours up.

COLIN: Yes, we did.

MIKE: How were the reviews?

COLIN: Very good. Excellent.

MIKE: I only saw the one in the Herald.

COLIN: That was the only bad one.

MIKE: Pity. That would've been the most important one for you.

COLIN: Not really.

MIKE: Meant to catch it. Didn't seem to be around long.

COLIN: It did eight weeks.

MIKE: Eight?

COLIN: If I'd wanted to run for a year I'd've written *E.T.*

MIKE: Won't be much return for the investors.

COLIN: We're hoping for an overseas sale.

MIKE: Wish you luck.

COLIN: The American reviewers seemed a bit cool to *Sister Nun.*

MIKE: Crying all the way to the bank. Had a six million U.S. presale.

COLIN: I read that you're cutting back on production.

MIKE: [*swallowing a tablet*] It's been tougher than we expected, but we're getting there.

COLIN: No plans for *Black Rage?*

MIKE: We've put that one on the back burner. Poor black kid making it is big news here, but it happens every day over there. Be hard for you to get a new movie up now, I suppose?

COLIN: It's always hard. Having problems with Equity I hear?

MIKE: Storm in a teacup.

COLIN: I heard they were axing your next movie unless at least one Australian got a lead role.

MIKE: They've got their head in the sand. How can I pre-sell our movies to the States with unknown actors in the lead? [*To the audience*] Why does the Film Commission invite him? Everyone in the industry knows his last film was a disaster. Eleven thousand in its first week and it went down from there. He'll be lucky if he ever gets another film up in his life, poor bastard. Can't help feeling sorry for him. I just wish the papers would start employing critics who like what the public like for a change, instead of giving losers like that the good crits.

COLIN: [*to the audience*] Why does the Commission keep inviting him? If he knew the contempt he was held in by all the people in this room, he'd never show his face around here again. I can't bring myself to hate him any more. He's a figure of great pathos. The only thing that makes me angry is the money he makes. I don't want to be rich, but it's sad to see the dollars go to turds like that, while *serious* film makers beg and scrape.

MIKE: Take care.

COLIN: You too.

> [MIKE *and* COLIN *nod at each other and turn away to face the audience. They stand there shaking their heads, assuming with never a doubt that the audience is on their side. As they share this certainty with the audience, the lights fade.*]

THE END